PINHOOK

OTHER BOOKS BY JANISSE RAY

Betweeen Two Rivers
EDITED WITH SUSAN CERULEAN AND LAURA NEWTON

Ecology of a Cracker Childhood

Naming the Unseen

Wild Card Quilt: Taking a Chance on Home

PINHOOK

Finding Wholeness in a Fragmented Land

Janisse Ray

CHELSEA GREEN PUBLISHING
WHITE RIVER JUNCTION, VERMONT

Project Editor: Collette Leonard
Developmental Editor: Robin Dutcher
Copy Editor: Robin Catalano
Proofreader: Laura Jorstad
Design and Composition: Peter Holm, Sterling Hill Productions
Map by Molly O'Halloran
Printed in Canada
First printing, February 2005
10 9 8 7 6 5 4 3 2 1

Printed on acid-free, 100 percent post-consumer waste recycled paper.

LIBRARY OF CONGRESS CATALOGING-IN-PUBLICATION DATA

Ray, Janisse, 1962-
Pinhook : finding wholeness in a fragmented land / by Janisse Ray.
    p. cm.
ISBN 1-931498-74-1
1. Natural history--Georgia--Pinhook Swamp. 2. Pinhook Swamp (Ga.) I.
Title.
QH105.G4R39 2005
508.758--dc22

                    2005000762

Chelsea Green Publishing Company
Post Office Box 428
White River Junction, Vermont 05001
Editorial and Sales Offices: (802) 295-6300
To place an order: (800) 639-4099
www.chelseagreen.com

*For all the people in the world
living in service to wildness,
and for those
working courageously and nonstop
to restore life.*

And for Raven.

CONTENTS

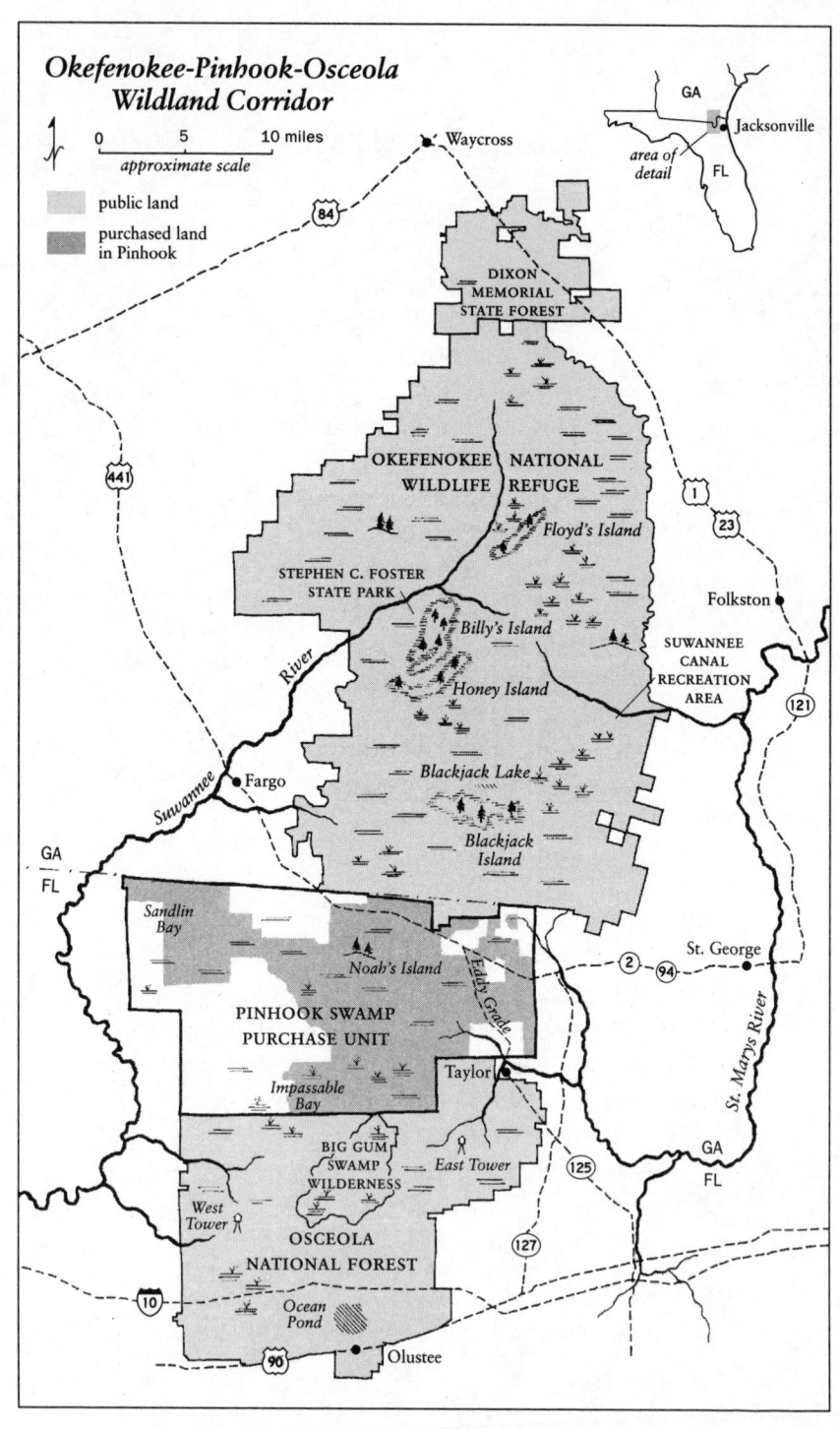

Okefenokee-Pinhook-Osceola Wildland Corridor

0   5   10 miles
approximate scale

public land

purchased land
in Pinhook

GA

Jacksonville

area of
detail

FL

Waycross

84

441

DIXON
MEMORIAL
STATE FOREST

1

23

OKEFENOKEE   NATIONAL
WILDLIFE   REFUGE

Floyd's Island

Folkston

STEPHEN C. FOSTER
STATE PARK

Billy's Island

SUWANNEE
CANAL
RECREATION
AREA

Honey Island

121

River

Blackjack Lake

Suwannee

Fargo

Blackjack
Island

GA
FL

Sandlin
Bay

Noah's Island

St. George

2

94

PINHOOK SWAMP
PURCHASE UNIT

Eddy Grade

St. Mary's River

Impassable
Bay

Taylor

BIG GUM
SWAMP
WILDERNESS

East Tower

125

GA
FL

West
Tower

OSCEOLA
NATIONAL
FOREST

127

10

Ocean
Pond

90

Olustee

INTRODUCTION

IN THE SOUTH of Georgia, endless pine flatwoods part to make way for a great swamp, Okefenokee, in whose thickets and bays lives a population of black bears so healthy that the straight, sandy roads of that territory are crossed and crisscrossed by the imprints of their pads. Often they are glimpsed at dusk, disappearing into titi thickets. The bears ignore a delineation drawn in 1819, after the Spaniards conceded, that marks the boundary of Florida. And they ignore Highway 94, which changes to Highway 2 at the state line, built to connect minuscule Fargo, Georgia, to equally small Saint George, Georgia, after passing briefly through a corner of Florida. The bears traverse freely through country mostly alien and uninhabitable for humans, where the world yet belongs to the processes of rain, sun, water, fire, and wind. The names of the places where they forage, they mate, they birth, and they nurse their young in the mysterious patterns of black-bear society are not the names we have given these locales: Grand Prairie, Sego Bay, Sandy Drain, Sawgrass Head, Little Suwannee. Knowledge of these places is contained permanently in a vast and secret black-bear culture.

Many miles south of the immense swamp, the one

named Okefenokee, lie the pine flatwoods of north-central Florida, interrupted by branches and bays, that we know as Osceola.

Okefenokee Swamp, Osceola National Forest.

The areas of these two wild lands, which are owned by the people of the United States, total more than half a million acres. Between them is a pocosin, connected to Okefenokee by sluggish Breakfast Branch and to Osceola by Impassable Bay.

We know it as Pinhook Swamp. The land between. The little bridge.

It is 170,000 acres of dreary dismal. A giant piece of ground too deep for a human to wade in, too shallow for a boat to draw. Too tangled for passage. Full of mosquitoes and yellow flies. A place that holds the world together. A natural feature full of natural features. Some of the last real wilderness in the South.

Pinhook's fate has been to be ignored, even unnamed. Not that it wasn't logged. Like most of the country, it was. But somehow Pinhook Swamp never lost its wild character, its mystery, its incomprehensibility, its elegance. The loggers logged and left. The trees returned.

Nobody knows much about it. Except the bears.

What if we bought Pinhook Swamp? What if we joined Osceola to Okefenokee? What if we preserved this "land between" for perpetuity? What if we added Moccasin Swamp to the east, Double Run Swamp to the west, Impassable Bay to the south? What if we dedicated ourselves to preserving and restoring a wild landscape, a corridor—O to O?

In the late 1980s that's what began to happen, patch by patch. And in 2001 the piece of the puzzle that finally connected Georgia to Florida ecologically, a heavily logged pine plantation owned by a timber company bordering Florida Highway 2, snapped into place.

The public-lands corridor was connected. Not complete, but not severed. Not broken. And the buyback continues.

I am not writing simply to describe this particular place, Pinhook Swamp, a pocosin neighboring grand wildness, but to tell you its story, the sad and happy of it. Because it is the back of a turtle, this story, on which many things can ride.

DAY

THE MORNING I first saw Pinhook was one of those tentative March days, before spring arrives in lustful earnest, when everything has a secret it bursts to tell. Some of the flora, unable to wait, has crept out of the tamped-down place it has been all winter, and in the calmness of a risk successfully executed, skips and dances bright colors across the land.

Clouds of yellow jessamine float among the tops of sapling trees, flame azalea sweep pink through the floodplains, fields are washed in sheep sorrel burgundies and toadflax lavenders. Red-shouldered hawks whistle over the bottomlands, and wild hogs root along the shoulders of the roads. Black willow catkins emerge yellow-green.

My husband, Raven, and I have driven from our family farm near the Altamaha River in Appling County, Georgia, about an hour north of Okefenokee Swamp, through the eagerness of spring. We have motored past houses and farms, one after another, past clear-cuts strung like giant beads on an awful necklace, past churches with their parking lots devoid of trees. We have driven through the little towns of south Georgia, Alma and Waycross and Homerville, with their attempts at industry and their

desires to grow. The entire route is so civilized, so human-
ized, so domesticated.

We are on our way to Olustee, Florida, where we are to
meet Larry Thompson, activist and longtime ally of Pinhook
Swamp. We will enter the wild pocosin from the Florida side.

The year has brought El Niño, and winter has been particularly cold and wet. For a month it has rained almost
daily—fifteen inches of precipitation in one month, a
quarter of the year's normal allotment. Winter has seemed
longer because of the rains, its gray chill extended. Rivers
are in tremendous flood, the water tannic and clean.
Ditches and creeks are so full they foam.

*Into the late 1800s the coastal plains of Georgia and Florida were a great
plate, engraved with sandhill crane, fox squirrel, spotted turtle, panther,
black bear. Diamondback rattlesnake, Suwannee bass, parrot pitcher
plant. Dusky seaside sparrow, snowy egret, red wolf. As humans arrived
they dictated their patterns onto a landscape that had been designed by
natural forces. Railroads came; trams were constructed into swamps.
Trees were severed from their roots, ditches were dug. Forests disappeared.
Savannas were plowed under.*

*Fragmentation is what happens when a glass platter falls. Except that
landscape fragmentation happens slowly, incrementally. In the moment
the first tree fell did the plate begin to slip? At what point did it lay broken
at our feet?*

Olustee, twelve miles west of Lake City, Florida, is famous
not for a bloody Civil War battle that occurred here but for
the annual reenactment of it. Mainly Olustee is a cross-
roads with a store, but it's home to the U.S. Forest Service

headquarters for the Osceola. By 10 A.M. we are inside the Forest Service, staring at a stuffed chuck-will's-widow and taxidermied raccoons fishing a polyurethane pond in front of a cypress swamp mural. Larry Thompson pulls open the glass door.

I met Larry more than a decade ago when I lived in Tallahassee. He was one of those people you have to know, a mover and shaker. I had recently experienced an epiphany. Life was good in my little hand-built cabin at the edge of a remnant Appalachian ravine, where in the pasture I grew persimmons and pears and tended a sprawling garden, and where I could live off the grid, free of consumer guilt. If I wanted to make a difference, however, if I wanted to inspire and educate others to honor wildness, I would have to venture forth into the world.

For twenty-three years Larry worked for the National Audubon Society in eight southeastern states, and in the last three years of his career was Florida's statewide organizer. I met him when I joined the board of the local Tallahassee chapter. Every year he led a bird-a-thon for our group—he collected pledges based on species of birds he and a few friends would see *in one day*. I learned not to pledge a dollar a species unless I wanted to donate at least a hundred and fifty bucks to Audubon.

Larry's nearing sixty, with hazel eyes and short-cropped brown hair. In 1985 he suffered a sort of personal earthquake, a brain tumor that took three operations, all more than fifteen hours long, to remove. This calamity crumpled one side of Larry's face, and is most evident in his left eye and in the way he appears to talk out of one side of his mouth.

You'd think he talks sideways on purpose, he's such a funny guy. He always has a joke. Everybody admires Larry for cheerfulness, for working with possibility instead of despair. Everybody enjoys his company.

This morning he has driven from his home in Tallahassee. These days he's devoting all his attention to Pinhook. "I don't know how long I have left," Larry had said to me. "I want to spend my time where I think I'll do the most good for wild things."

The office manager buzzes William Metz, current district ranger of the Osceola, with news of our arrival, and Will strides from the back—tall, open-faced, healthy, all smiles. He's very tan for an administrator, his eyes a clear blue-green. He invites us to his office, which is like a greenhouse, it has so many plants. It has maps on the walls and a computer at the desk. A head-high ficus tree in a pot catches light from the open window. Will spreads open on his desk an oversized map.

"Here is the boundary of Osceola," he says. "And this, up here, is where Okefenokee Swamp begins. This in-between is Pinhook. Highway 2 runs here." He swishes his finger across the paper.

"Highway 2 was built on what some pundit called the Blue Ridge," says Larry.

"The Blue Ridge?"

"It's a narrow interfluve, as they say, that separates Pinhook from the Okefenokee. It's no more than ten feet above the swamps, in most places less than five. I'm sure that before it was a highway, even a dirt road, it was an Indian trail."

Will points to a block in the center of the map. "The first piece to be purchased was this." He and Larry start talking acquisitions so quickly I can't follow. "This was the last purchase." He points to one next to Okefenokee. I'm studying the map, blocks of mint green (government), blocks of pink (still privately owned).

"So Osceola and Okefenokee actually touch?" I ask.

"Yes," Larry answers, "we have the corridor."

Suddenly Will glances at the window. Outside there is sunshine. We've been cooped up by El Niño. "You can get this information from papers," he says. "Let's just go see Pinhook."

He packs us into his sea-green Forest Service Jeep and heads east, stopping to fill up with gasoline at the convenience store that marks the one caution light in Olustee. We traipse in for bottles of water and bags of cheddar popcorn. Two old gentlemen are gassing up a pickup whose bed is loaded with bags of trash. One of them speaks to Will in a southern dialect so strong I don't understand him at first, and Will doesn't either. He asks the man to repeat, and stands listening, smiling in a friendly fashion.

"Bream bitin' at Ocean Pon'," the man tells him. "Late de evening."

"Oh," Will says. "Okay. Great. I'm ready for some fishing."

"They bitin' wums."

"I've got to get out there. Fishing's what I need. Thanks."

We turn north from the gas station and travel a long way through national forest. We're really in the country, tall pines all around, no signs of human occupation. Oh, glory. This land is our land. We cross the Saint Marys River, which runs from Okefenokee Swamp to the Atlantic Ocean. We pass East Tower, used for spotting forest fires, then cruise through tiny Taylor, Florida, with its teensy Voting House, two soda machines out front, and its toy fire department, community playground out back. After many miles we veer onto Eddy Grade.

Although the maps call Eddy Grade an "improved road," it is sandy dirt and pitted with potholes. Frequently it is eroded by troughs of tannic water, created by overflowing swamp on either side. The full ditches are big enough to be called creeks. Now, most of what we're passing through is Forest Service land that is not forest at all, but cutover pineland replanted in rows of slash pines, all about twelve feet tall.

"This was a recent acquisition," Will says.

"It has been logged many times," Larry says. By 1898 the railroad connecting Valdosta, Georgia, to Jacksonville, Florida, was completed, and areas between Okefenokee and Pinhook were logged for the first time at the turn of the twentieth century. At that time the view from the train, I have read, was a landscape of stumps. Intense logging was taking place deep in Pinhook Swamp in the 1930s. It has continued to this day, since the landowners of Pinhook have been timber companies. Pinhook was company land, an industrial landscape superimposed on a rare wild one.

"Timber companies wanted to log, sell, and get the hell out of the lowlands," Larry continues. "We want to help them get out."

After some time we turn again onto a sodden road barely wide enough for the vehicle, and drive out into the swamp along a tram built to haul logs out of Pinhook. It is as straight as a Southern Baptist deacon. The tram has not been used recently enough to wear tracks in the brown grass that grows along it, now waterlogged, nor to keep the flanking vegetation at bay.

"Look carefully along the road," Will says. "We should see an alligator." The deeper holes in the ditches are their wallows. Will wants very badly to show us an alligator, as if this has become Wild Adventures and he's our guide. He is not a native Floridian, not even a southerner. The Forest Service has moved him from pillar to post, from island to forest to desert to swamp. We assure him that we've viewed plenty of alligators, some up close, but Will knows that alligators persuade. They're big, their lives depend on places like Pinhook Swamp, they're wild, they've adapted, and they could eat you (if they were hungry enough to surmount their fear of bipedal creatures).

A Suwannee cooter drops off a log protruding from a shallow pond.

"A turtle!" Will exclaims. "Did you see that?"

Fragmentation is the separation of habitat in a landscape. It means chopping a wild place into pieces, or slicing bites off its edges, or putting a road or other divider through the heart of it so that it becomes a conglomerate of smaller, less functional pieces. In simple math fragmentation is long division. Anytime a human construct—house, building, field, road, parking lot, power line, pipeline, mine, clear-cut, food plot, canal, levee, embankment—destroys anything of nature, it fragments the landscape. Even a thing as insubstantial as a fence or a footpath serves to partition the landscape and significantly alter the abundance and behavior of certain species. Inholdings (developed tracts) within a natural area diminish the forest from within. Industrial and urban development destroy, modify, or degrade natural habitat.

Fragmentation usually proceeds along a continuum that ranges from intact, functional habitat to a fragmented forest, then an archipelago of forest patches in a sea of development, and finally to a single, isolated piece of desperately salvaged natural habitat. We see fragmentation mostly from airplanes. Fly over Orlando or Anchorage or Pittsburgh or Mexico City and you will see landscapes broken and pierced, so much that almost none of them remain as they were. Flying over British Columbia, where logging is intense, the primeval forest, kept wild and unbroken until so recently, is down to naught in places. Double ought. Even flying at twenty thousand feet the clear-cuts are mammoth pocks.

Sometimes rivers are channeled and do not run where they once did or where they would if humans had not disrupted the course of history. Sometimes wild lands are fragmented by pollution, by dioxins and arsenic and fecal coliform, and sometimes by land mines and other explosives. Sometimes by oil spills. By the depleted uranium used in bullets and missiles, dropped onto war lands. By nuclear testing and nuclear waste.

"You've heard of greenbelts?" asks Larry. "Greenbelts make most folks happy. People want what they call open space in urban areas, such as rails-to-trails, river walks, small parks. Pinhook is not a greenway. This is one large, functioning ecosystem, unparalleled in the Southeast."

"Corridors of the last resort," I say.

He pauses and turns in the front seat enough that I can see his devilish grin. "A greenway is to a wildlife corridor what a Venetian is to a venetian blind," Larry says. "This is habitat."

We're motoring slowly enough to hear a pig frog calling, *oink oink*. Duck potato, a native perennial, spears up through the ditches, blooming white triangles with yellow centers, like little kites flying on green tethers above the popping water. We spook a great egret. We see a slate-blue bird looking for an easy meal in a shallow pool. Larry calls it a B. B. King bird.

"They're singing the blues," he says. It's a little blue heron.

Really not many birds are flying and singing, since migration has not fully begun. But it's spring now and the songbirds will be coming back from even more southerly parts, hauling the sun on their backs. Pinhook has been designated an "Important Bird Area" by the American Bird Conservancy.

"You know you're a real birder," Larry says, "when someone yells, 'Duck!' and you stand up and say, 'Where?'" Larry leads bird-watching trips—most of his clients are older, he says, like himself. They can't duck. If you let them get down on the ground, they can't get back up.

I spy an unusual patch of spangle far ahead on the tram, a quarter mile away. We journey toward it slowly, on account of the state of the path. "Is that a deer?"

How many times have I longed for eyes of kingfishers, clarity despite distance, able to see minnows in the cloudy tides of salt creeks? Or for those of wild turkeys, who know which speck in the heavens is a hawk instead of a buzzard? I rely deeply on binoculars. They are difficult to focus in motion, but I bring them up now. It *is* a deer. Closer we are able to ascertain, unaided, a doe's blurry outline blending with brush. She waves her flag of peace and disappears off the road. Wherever she is, her hooves are wet, and she presses greenery apart to make room for her body.

After a long time Will turns once more. Walls of vegetation crowd us, smothering the brimming ditches. Brush beats the sides of the car and sometimes whips through the open windows to pop and sting our arms.

"Watch your eyes," Will says. The Jeep has been in four-wheel drive since Eddy Grade. In some places the streaming water has trenched out a gully deep enough to jolt the vehicle's suspension system and slam its underparts against the ground. Soon, happily, there will again be no road here. Occasionally Will glances in the rearview mirror, a bright twinkle in his eye, to see how we are doing with all the pitching and bumping. I can tell he's afraid of getting us stuck out in Pinhook Swamp, and on the other hand, it's the thing he most wants.

Finally the passage widens a bit, enough to gingerly turn around, which Will does, inching up and back by degrees. "This is as far as we should go," he says, apologetically. "We all have scheduled afternoons."

Not all fragmentation is human-caused: Hurricane Andrew screamed through the pine rocklands of southern Florida in 1992. A series of tornadoes touched down near Camilla, Georgia, in 2002. Lightning-set fires helped burn an unprepared Yellowstone in 1988.

But if you look around through the eyes of an industrialist or a consumer or a city dweller (forgive me, all you ecological urbanites), you see what mortals have created: the fruits of human genius. You see the pride of roads, the ingenuity of skyscrapers, the capability of cathedrals, the hubris of parks, the skill of bridges. But if you look at land through the eyes of a naturalist, or outdoorsperson, or veery, or striped newt, or red fox, you see greater and greater sections closed: For most wild animals, there is no food, no shelter, no water, no safety, and no sense of home in a parking lot.

Once, on a colossal balance, humanity's footprint hardly trembled the scale when weighed against the tremendous, powerful, awe-inspiring, death-fearsome world of nature. Oh, glorious wild nature. Now we are grinding it down to nothing.

Will cuts the engine and disembarks. We pile out into the bright early-spring sunshine, four people unleashed in an unscrolling, unbridled wilderness, onto one contiguous mat of green and water. The sunshine is not yet saffron, not even full lemon yellow, but a weak colorlessness, as if the Carolina jessamine extracts most of the available gold from the air.

Will has been quiet so far, absorbed in driving and in his search for wildlife. He has answered any question I've asked, but has volunteered little to no information on his own. In open air he transforms.

"This is the heart of the Pinhook," he announces grandly. He gestures excitedly, master of ceremony. "This is what the Pinhook is all about." He becomes charged, buoyant, even oratorical. "It's functional. It's intact. The processes and structure are here as they should be. This is one last rare, intact, functioning ecosystem." I smile to myself because Will's argument sounds like a verse of rap. I look out over the forgotten pocosin.

"I love this place because it's not the Everglades," Will says. He bounces a few steps and stretches his arms wide. "It doesn't need to be restored." He gets a look that says *That's all there is to convey, really.*

At first I assume his is the happiness of an administrator who, first inspired by love of the outdoors, after much desk work is turned loose anew in the wild world. Will's behavior, however, is something else I struggle to recognize.

Pinhook reminds me too of the Everglades—wet, expansive, savannalike. I can see that the land, at least this spring, is one flowing sheet of water, like the 'Glades. The water moves east, I will learn, toward the Middle Prong of the Saint Marys River, which pours out its banks across the shady, lovely, palmetto-and-wild-azalea bottomlands, joining sheets of water. The water travels through the pine flatwoods like it hasn't done in at least a decade, with the cleansing avail of a flood.

But Will is wrong. Pinhook does need restoration. Maybe not here, where the shrub-bog is intact, but to get here we have driven through miles of unnatural pine plantations, planted on raised beds of dirt. All that, the body of Pinhook, will have to be returned to the way it was.

Here in the heart of Pinhook the principal ground cover is a head-tall snarl of shrubs, instead of the sawgrass of the 'Glades. I climb atop the Jeep for a better look. Around us the vegetation—titi and myrtle and fetterbush and gallberry—is broken occasionally by a slash or a pond pine. Pond pines are new to me. They retain needles much farther down their trunks than other pines. They're scrawnier, shorter. The sky is wide open; full of clouds; uninterrupted by power lines, buildings, and billboards; waiting for a painter. Larry has spotted a mockingbird.

"Mockingbird? I can see one of them in a parking lot," I tease him from the vehicle roof. "Where are the sandhill cranes and the wood storks?"

"I wish I could call them up," he replies. "I'd make a lot more money for the bird-a-thons." I click a couple of pictures of Larry, binoculars raised. "But they're here, even if we don't see them."

Pinhook Swamp is serenely beautiful in an aloof kind of way. It's like a whale so ancient and so colossal and so fulfilled by its own life that it cares nothing of yours. Pinhook does not sweep out its green arms to embrace you. It doesn't even look your way, though you turn and marvel and ooh and click your camera this way and that: more or less sky, trees framing the distance or taking center stage, more or less light. In the macro, time-lapse field of blindness, the white fists of fetterbush open. Bees lick pollen off the five stamens inside a jessamine's throat. Tongue of sundew closes around a gnat. A field of water flies eastward.

How can it be that humans have lived in the southeastern coastal plain for twelve thousand years and sandhill cranes for sixty million years, and cranes have never built one supercenter or landfill or football stadium?

They dance in the sphagnum bogs.

Why haven't we figured out by now, with all this potential human evolution, how to live without so much alteration, so much fragmentation? The world is a globe of leaf-green continents amid five blue-green oceans, land we knife into smaller and smaller scraps.

I have been writing as if to suggest that all of Pinhook has been tucked away inside a safe-deposit box, and now we can rest easy, assured our retirement is secure.

I have misled you.

"When you say Pinhook Swamp, people either have never heard of it or they say, 'Oh, that's been saved already!'" says Larry. "It hasn't been saved. We have a contiguous corridor, but we figure only 70 percent of the area has been protected.

"Once you get 70 percent saved, between state and federal ownership," Larry continues, "the danger is, you think, This is wonderful, and you quit. You say, 'I'm so far ahead I'm going to take a rest.' You say, 'We've got over half. Let's not worry about the other half.' No. We have to worry about the other half. Pinhook is still easily purchasable. We're not talking about private tracts of land. Those are timberlands. These were lands that a hundred years ago no one wanted.

Wastelands. This is not hundreds of landowners. Only a few. Now's the time to buy it, while it's still relatively uninhabited."

I don't interrupt him. "I admit this is a lofty goal," he says. "We have the chance here to do something really grand. Are we going to let this area die the death of a thousand cuts?" Larry is full of proverbs. "One more, one more, one more? No, let's protect one more, one more. The way to eat an elephant is one bite at a time."

I gaze around and around and around, then look back at Larry. He is focused far out in the distance, toward the scribbled horizon.

"A few million would purchase the remainder of Pinhook and keep it in good condition for eternity. That's a small investment, to sustain life and society down here in Florida. If we can get Pinhook saved, we're going to look back and realize it was a major good thing." Larry pauses. "I'm afraid what people don't value, they don't keep. And most people don't understand the wonder of a large ecosystem like this."

Larry goes silent, and I look to see what Will is thinking. He seems happy, ringed by pocosin, eating saltines. I raise the camera and he becomes boisterous. He sticks a cracker in each ear and grins. Then he removes them, hides the package behind his back, and waits for the picture, the bog at his back. I understand then his behavior. It is sheer, wild elation, a strange joy to simply be in a place like this.

Fragmentation is what happens when an argument breaks out at a family reunion, over what to do with joint property or the biracial marriage of a nephew, and years pass before the family meets again. A family feud or an argument between old friends is fragmentation.

War is fragmentation between countries. Fragmentation is the Iraqi man who lost ten members of his family in the 2003 U.S. attack on his country. Ten in one family. He is encircled by coffins, all of which hold members of his now-dead family, and he is moving from one to another, saying good-bye. The photograph in the newspaper shows him weeping over the coffin of his mother. Many times, I'm certain, the man wonders why he had been called away from home.

Fragmentation lives next door to annihilation.

The worst part of fragmentation is that it leads to isolation. For humans isolation is the place of hopelessness, of depression, of despair. By deduction, then, we know community to be a place of hope, of possibility, of wholeness. Human community, wild community.

What can I know of Pinhook? Few have explored or studied this nether-country. There is little we can read about it. Visitors and locals have forayed into it, prospecting or moonshining or hunting or looking for lost dogs, but none has approached the heart of Pinhook Swamp. Neither can I. I can see it with my eyes, from the vantage of a car top along a tram. I can hear its flies buzz and its red-bellied woodpeckers pound against fire-dead pines. But I can go no farther. I must stand, gazing at the tangled low-country, and know it to be the unknown: a land of secrets, a place untamed. It is a continent beyond us.

LAY OF THE LAND

IT IS IMPORTANT to pause briefly to understand why things are the way they are. Which is history.

OSCEOLA was proclaimed a national forest on July 10, 1931. It is 158,225 acres, managed by the U.S. Department of Agriculture's Forest Service.

OKEFENOKEE, the largest freshwater swamp in the United States (not counting the Everglades and Atchafalaya), currently covers 438,000 acres, or 660 square miles. In the late 1830s the last of its Creek and Seminole inhabitants were killed or ousted, and until 1889 it belonged to the people of Georgia. In that year Georgia sold the swamp to the Suwannee Canal Company for fourteen and a half cents an acre; Atlanta capitalist Harry Jackson intended to drain it. That project died with Jackson, and in 1908 the swamp was sold to Hebard Lumber Company, which proceeded to log it. In the late 1930s Jean Harper, wife of naturalist Francis Harper, who first entered the swamp with a Cornell University biological expedition in May 1912 and who returned to live for months at a time with his family there, beseeched President Franklin D. Roosevelt to purchase Okefenokee Swamp in order to spare it. Jean Harper was an acquaintance of the president, having tutored his children. In 1937 Roosevelt declared Okefenokee Swamp a national wildlife refuge, to be managed by the Department of the Interior's Fish and Wildlife Service. Ninety percent of Okefenokee, a portion of which extends into Florida, is official wilderness, the largest area east of the Mississippi.

Connected to Okefenokee on its north end is 35,708-acre DIXON MEMORIAL STATE FOREST, encompassing 15,000 acres of the swamp around the area of Cowhouse Island. Dixon, a wildlife management area, is managed by the Georgia Forestry Commission. The state forest, purchased in 1955, contains about 1,200 acres of natural pine stands, 2,000 to 3,000 acres of hardwood bottomlands, and 18,000 acres of planted pine. The timber is cut in forty-year rotations, 250 to 300 acres a year, with no cut bigger than 70 acres. Laura S. Walker State Park, deeded to the Georgia Department of Natural Resources, is entirely within the boundaries of the state forest—it is devoted to recreation and includes a golf course.

So Dixon is cut. So it contains a golf course. Bears breed there in the heads and thickets. If Dixon Memorial State Forest is wild enough for bears, it's wild enough for me.

Osceola's 158,225 plus Okefenokee's 438,000 equals 596,225. Add Dixon's 35,708 and the total is 631,933. Count what's saved so far in Pinhook—about 120,000 acres—and we have a wild land corridor with a grand total of 751,933 acres.

Seven hundred fifty-one thousand nine hundred thirty-three acres. Heading toward a million. Bigger than the land area of Rhode Island. A million acres for river otters, black-crowned night herons, hoary bats, two-toed amphiumas, eastern chicken turtles, round-tailed muskrats, and Cooper's hawks. For sandhill cranes and black bears. For the possibility of red wolves, whooping cranes, and Florida panthers.

Pinhook models a large contiguous conservation corridor for the nation. O to O. O2O.

Give me a moment here to applaud, to whoop and holler, to skip out from behind my writing desk and do a little dance in the study.

I'd like to get to the middle of all that ground and lie down and rest awhile.

Holding the World Together

A POCOSIN IS a tract of low swamp, usually wooded, a shrubby bog that inherits its name from the Algonquian word *poquo*, meaning "to open out or widen." It's also called a *dismal*, or a "swamp on a hill."

Most of Pinhook is dismal.

Walk out into the pocosin and you will sink to your knees in a peaty muck. Fetterbush, or hurrah bush, tugs at you, and the vicious smilax, or greenbriar, threatens to tear out your eyes and hair. For a while you can fight your way through gallberry, titi, more than one kind of native blueberry, and Virginia willow. Stop and lather up your hands with poor man's soap (sweet pepperbush), which foams when rubbed with wet hands.

Each step will leave a mark in the mats of sphagnum, which grow thick and wide, happy with constant inundation. Far above the shrubs you will see an occasional slash pine or the more unusual pond pine.

You won't go far before you have to beat a not-so-hasty retreat.

Pocosins are defined by a flat topography, a hydrology driven by rainfall, and organic, peaty soils. Waters typically flow outward from the center of pocosins, eventually forming headwaters of streams near the outer boundaries. Because organic soils tend to hold water longer than mineral soils, pocosins traditionally burned much less often than upland forests, or every fifteen to thirty years. Even so, fire is essential to this community; it prevents the formation of a closed-canopy wetland.

Pocosins and their counterparts, Carolina bays, the mystifying tear-shaped depressions oriented northwest–southeast that occur in the sandy soils of the southeastern coastal plains, originally made up about three and a half million acres in North and South Carolina and Georgia. Less than one-third of them are intact; another third have been irrevocably altered. Most pocosins and Carolina bays have been converted to farmland, tree plantations (bedded pines), or peat mines. The southernmost Carolina bays can be found in the environs of Pinhook. Pocosins are critical breeding sites for amphibians.

The southeastern United States has a higher number of endangered ecosystems than any other region of the country. More than 30 percent are critically endangered.

Crisscrossed through the pocosin are strands, bays, and pockets of true swamp, forested by loblolly bay, black gum, red maple, sweet bay, and pond cypress. Some of these are cypress domes, called so because older, taller trees grow in the middle, with younger trees to the outside. Occasionally the pocosin pauses for savannas, which are wet, grassy prairies maintained by periodic fires in dry years. Wet prairies are often green with Virginia chain fern and rush, and comely with pitcher plants, sedges, bladderworts, green arum, rose pogonia, maiden cane, red root, and sphagnum.

Slash and pond pines grow in the wet pinewoods, above the familiar understory of saw palmetto, gallberry, fetterbush, scattered wax myrtle, tarflower, and dangleberry. In the highest and driest pinewoods, longleaf pine may be found, although it probably was never a common species. The majority of Pinhook's pinewoods have been converted to slash pine plantations, and many portions were drained, logged, and replanted with row crops of trees.

The Florida Natural Areas Inventory named drainage of wetlands the greatest threat to Pinhook Swamp. According to the U.S. Geological Survey, the United States originally contained almost 392 million acres of wetlands. Of that, about 105 million acres remain. The loss is attributed to urban sprawl, agriculture, silvicultural conversion, and rural development. No state has lost less than 20 percent of its wetlands; Florida alone lost about 9.3 million acres in the two hundred years between the 1780s and the 1980s. (California has lost the most wetlands, more than 90 percent.) Between 1986 and 1997, the rate of destruction slowed 80 percent, to a loss of 58,500 acres annually.

Wide floodplains, extensive coastal plains, and plenty of rainfall have created in the Southeast a region rich in wetlands. About 47 percent of the country's wetlands occur in the southeastern states. Possibly half of Florida and Louisiana may have originally been wetlands.

Forested wetlands, a class of native land that includes pocosins, cypress domes, and floodplain swamps, suffered the greatest countrywide decline of any wetland type. These ecosystems declined countrywide 16 percent between the 1950s and 1970s, when government protection began. This equaled 276,000 acres per year. Between the '70s and '80s more than 3.1 million acres of forested wetlands were destroyed in one way or another in the Southeast; the decline was 345,000 acres per year. Now fewer than 50 million acres of forested wetland remain. Keystone species that indicate the function of forested wetlands, like swallow-tailed kites, cerulean warblers, and Swainson's warblers, continue to decline.

Unsurprisingly, Pinhook Swamp supports historic civilizations of river otter, bobcat, mink, weasel, gray fox, sandhill crane, migratory waterfowl, and swallow-tailed kite, species associated with the rich wetlands of the South. Most people, however, would wade a few feet into the muck and conclude that Pinhook Swamp isn't good for much besides holding the world together.

THE NAME

HOW DID PINHOOK get its name? Here is more mystery. The word has no written meaning. Slender hook on which to hang clothes? The piece that holds the rest together? Wooden nail that secures a wilderness saved from our fiercely curious, infinitely reaching human brains?

Florida was acquired from Spain and admitted as a U.S. territory in 1819, and as a state in 1845. But the boundary between Georgia and Florida was not officially run until 1859. The U.S.-Spanish border had been agreed upon in 1799 to 1800 following a survey by Andrew Ellicott for the United States and a Captain Minor for the Spanish. Spain and the United States had agreed that the boundary stretched from the confluence of the Chattahoochee and Flint rivers to the point where the Saint Marys River left the Okefenokee Swamp. The men had been unable to run the line because of the resistance of the Native people to having their lands taken, but managed to canoe up the Saint Marys River and erect a small mound at the point they agreed that the Saint Marys left the Okefenokee. This became known as Ellicott's Mound.

Until 1842 the army was much involved in suppressing Seminole unrest in the area. In November 1838 U.S.

general Charles R. Floyd and his army patrols passed along the northern rim of Pinhook on a reconnaissance. Floyd ordered regular patrolling of the area, and in 1840 the U.S. Army established a fort northwest of the pocosin. Their reports never mention Pinhook by name.

Meanwhile, the U.S. Army Corp of Engineers were more involved in building forts, roads, and bridges than in measuring the new lands, and since few white people were moving in, the project lacked urgency. Then Florida was admitted as a state in 1845. Georgia and Florida couldn't agree on the line.

Two Floridians surveyed the Georgia-Florida boundary in the summer of 1854, camping the nights of July 18 and 19 west of Breakfast Branch on the Blue Ridge. They did not call Pinhook by name.

The survey party of Richard L. Hunter crossed between Okefenokee and Pinhook around New Year's Day in 1857. His men did not call the place Pinhook. One of the surveyors, Miller B. Grant, noted accounts of wolves attacking wild cattle and reports of panthers in the area.

Finally Georgia and Florida appointed Gustavus Orr and B. F. Whitner Jr. to establish a boundary between the states. The men began at the Chattahoochee River and ran eastward, missing Ellicott's Mound by twenty-four feet. Their work was accepted by the United States in 1860.

In 1878 to 1879 S. L. Fremont, employee of the U.S. Army Corps of Engineers, surveyed a proposed ship canal from the Saint Marys River to the Gulf of Mexico. The lasting contribution of this survey is the placement on the subsequent map of Okefenokee in a regional context, detailing its relationship to the large pocosin to the south. Fremont's "Map of the Country" shows large areas labeled as OPEN PRAIRIE and refers to Pinhook as BAY SWAMP. The cartographer labeled the landscape UNEXPLORED and IMPENETRABLE.

Likely, therefore, the name *Pinhook* originated in the twentieth century. Someone told me that *Pinhook* was the name of a man who had once bought the north Florida pocosin, which doesn't fit and I could not verify. Someone said the place was named after the parasitic worm. That's also mistaken—the parasites are *pin*worm and *hook*worm. A fishing hook made from a straight pin has been called a "pinhook."

My friend Milton Hopkins, who has spent over fifty years farming near Osierfield, Georgia, wrote me in a letter: "Back when we were growing over twenty acres of tobacco we all hated to hear the word 'pinhook' on a tobacco auction for it meant the unsavory group of guys from North Carolina had come out onto the sale floor looking for bargains. Even legitimate tobacco buyers looked down on these guys." According to Milton, when farmers sold their cured tobacco, company buyers followed a hasty auctioneer around a warehouse filled with bundles of tobacco. If a buyer bid on a sheet and then pulled out a handful of molded tobacco from the middle of the sheet, he turned it down. The auctioneer resold the tobacco immediately for sometimes one-tenth of the original bid.

"That's when the 'pinhookers' stepped in and bought the sheet for a little of nothing," Milton wrote, "hooked their pinhook onto the oak basket and slid it across the concrete several rows ahead of the sale. Pinhookers always kept several men or women hired to hastily re-sort the sheet, picking out any suspect leaves." They then resold the tobacco for several hundred times their bid.

Timber pinhookers worked on the same principle.

Milton drew a picture of a pinhook—a metal rod with a curved end, attached to a perpendicular wooden handle. "Pinhook Swamp," he wrote, "may be the hell all pinhookers went to heaven."

Florida also has a Pinhook River, in the Saint Marks Wildlife Refuge, but no official trace of the word's origin can be found.

Mr. Pinhook's folly? A pinhooked land deal? Place of corporeal parasites? Tool with a hook? Place that pins the world together?

NATIVE BLESSING

LET US PUT our minds together and give thanks
for the life we've been given,
for the chance to dream and wake and go out
among the meadow beauty, raising its many
velvet faces toward the sun.
For the cypress standing in sleepy congregations
like cloaked women in prayer.
For cubbyholes and cavities, grass beds and hollow
tupelos, for branch forks and underbanks.
For the open throats of pitcher plants
singing like bog frogs in the dusk.
For wild persimmon and huckleberry and hickory nut,
cattail and Ogeechee lime.
For reefs of flowers sweetly exhaling.
For beakers of rain poured liberally
from an archangel sky, the alchemy of rivers and bogs.
And thank the lightning that sparks heaven's love for earth,
conductor of fire.
Let us put our minds together and give thanks
for all the two-leggeds and four-leggeds and six-leggeds,
the many-leggeds and the no-leggeds,
near to far.

Let us especially thank the two who gave us life.
And thank Mother Earth, Elder Brother Sun,
   Grandmother
Moon, Sister Stars. Families. Safe Journeys.

Let us put our minds together and give thanks.

History of Acquisitions

IN LATE 1984 in a paper he delivered at a workshop called "Technologies to Benefit Agriculture and Wildlife," Florida biologist Larry D. Harris first proposed the Pinhook Corridor. His outline to the U.S. Congress's Office of Technology Assessment used the Suwannee River as a backbone for a body of land that joined Okefenokee to Osceola, and then connected them via the river to the Lower Suwanee National Wildlife Refuge on the Gulf Coast. Harris deplored the many agencies that, although tasked with preserving the biological heritage of our country, worked against each other in the practical application of their mission. He called for comprehensive planning on a vast scale in order to create "meaningful landscape mosaics consisting of habitat islands and abundant travel and dispersal corridors." Nothing less would stem the hemorrhaging of wild things from the planet.

In 1988 Congress authorized the Forest Service to begin buying Pinhook Swamp. This move came at the urging of Carol Browner, head of the Florida Department of Environmental Protection (whom President Clinton would later appoint to head the U.S. Department of Environmental Protection and who would serve the longest term in that position), and George Willson, director of land acquisition of The Nature Conservancy of Florida (later vice president for conservation of St. Joe Development Company). The Forest Service's "purchase unit" included 170,600 acres of Pinhook Swamp and its environs, to be bought with dollars from the Land and Water Conservation Fund (LWCF).

LWCF revenues for land acquisition are earned from oil and gas leases. At least 40 percent of LWCF money must go toward federal land acquisition and is split among four agencies—national parks, national forests, national wildlife refuges, and the Bureau of Land Management. The rest goes to states for outdoor recreation areas. Legislators annually authorize how the funds are spent. So a lot of lobbying goes on. House and Senate subcommittees list their priorities for land acquisitions (as part of the overall Interior appropriations bill), a proposal that goes on a harrowing journey through red tape until finally reaching a conference that settles differences between the House and Senate wishes. Then it proceeds to the president's desk to be signed into law. Since President Bush took office, LWCF allocations have seriously declined.

In 1988 following congressional approval of the Pinhook project, The Nature Conservancy immediately purchased thirty-four thousand acres, which the Forest Service bought back as funds were available. Between 1992 and 1997, Congress approved $7.38 million to buy Pinhook. If enough money could not be found to buy the entire swamp at once, then the visionaries would buy it back year by year, patch by patch. Public lands in Pinhook grew. But as the years passed, enthusiasm for its protection dwindled. Legislators didn't want to keep shoveling funds to some godforsaken Florida swamp.

In 1997 Pinhook got five hundred thousand dollars.
In 1998 Pinhook got nothing.

Corridors are natural habitats that link pieces of forest or other wild lands. Antidotes to fragmentation, they allow dispersal and movement of animals between habitats within their home ranges; into depopulated areas, for the purpose of resettlement; and into additional tracts, in order to colonize them. When hunting and other disturbances wipe out a local population of black bears, for example, corridors allow the bears to recolonize from a habitat with a thriving black-bear society. Grass and wildflower corridors connecting isolated meadows translate into increased numbers of butterflies, including cloudless sulphurs, common buckeyes, and spicebush swallowtails, as well as other insects. Corridors aid juvenile red-cockaded woodpeckers with dispersal.

Yet we must be careful when we use the word corridor. *We think of hallways in schools and hospitals, twelve feet wide. As many scientists have argued, narrow beltways do not benefit every species. Some wild species that thrive in a variety of habitats are unaffected by corridors. And when parcels of intact habitat become too small, not even corridors between habitats can rescue the inhabitants. For a corridor to be of utmost service, it should provide the accoutrements for a creature's survival, not just conveyance. Corridors are not wild highways. They are blanks filled in.*

Year after year, the Southern Region of the Forest Service put Pinhook Swamp first on its list of priority acquisitions. Every step of the way people wrote letters to their legislators on behalf of Pinhook. They made phone calls to Washington, faxed memos. Year after year the Pinhook project received no congressional funding.

"How can it stay a priority with no funding?" Larry asks.

"It's not getting congressional support. So internal enthusiasm is drying up."

In 2001 the state of Florida purchased 57,329 acres that were considered to be the missing piece of the puzzle, a pine plantation heavily logged most recently by Rayonier, Inc. It more than doubled all that had been purchased in Pinhook so far. Florida named the tract the John Bethea State Forest and began negotiations to sell it to the Forest Service. To have all of Pinhook protected under one federal agency was everybody's goal. When Congress passed the Interior appropriations bill without mention of Pinhook Swamp, the National Wildlife Federation lobbied for inclusion, which resulted in Congress agreeing that one million dollars be spent to purchase another thousand acres of Pinhook.

Pinhook's LWCF status for acquisition fell from number one to number eight. It got nothing from the government coffers. And President Bush later chopped the Forest Service budget.

"This will drop off the radar screen," says Larry. "It dies the death of neglect."

In 2003 the last piece of the puzzle connecting Georgia to Florida ecologically was added to the Forest Service; a section of John Bethea State Forest bordering Florida Highway 2 became federal lands. The piece was converted from clear-cutting on 15- to 20-year rotations to selective harvesting on a 100- to 120-year cycle.

Florida is in the process of trading the federal government deeds to about eighteen thousand acres of land in Pinhook for land and mineral rights the feds own (on two state forests and a number of other state-owned lands). The state gets mineral rights, and another large chunk of land in the wildland corridor comes under the management of the Forest Service. This will protect Pinhook from phosphate mining, since land in Osceola National Forest, per a law passed in Florida by Governor Lawton Chiles in the early 1980s, is out of reach of phosphate companies.

In early 2004 the Suwannee River Water Management District owned 12,559 acres in Pinhook that it had purchased with the understanding that the Forest Service would buy it back. The state of Florida still owned acreage as well. Through various means, including the use of mitigation funds, these public lands are being transferred into federal ownership.

A problem has been the infighting of government agencies. Buying land should be any conservation agency's top priority, and agencies should be able to work together to manage a natural system. We the people own the water management district, we own the Forest Service, we own the state of Florida. What does it matter that one arm of our government struggles to find the money to hand to another arm? Isn't the vision for wildness held commonly? Would the Suwannee River Water Management District, in order to recoup the money it spent in Pinhook, sell its parcels *back* to a development or timber company? Really.

While we all agree that federal ownership makes for more streamlined management and greater protection for Pinhook Swamp, the ultimate objective must be preservation.

To date a total of 120,000 acres of Pinhook Swamp have been placed in public ownership for safekeeping. (Most of that is now titled to the federal government.)

When completed, O2O will become one of the largest protected wildlife corridors east of the Mississippi.

THE MINE

IN 1997 I returned to live in my hometown in south Georgia. I had been away for seventeen years, most recently in Montana, learning to write and to be an activist. With trepidation I reinhabited my homeland, a poor region that scrimped on environmental thinking. In fact, when I returned I landed in the middle of a seemingly winless fight.

DuPont Corporation was riveting national attention on Okefenokee Swamp. Their proposal, broached in 1997, was to mine titanium from Trail Ridge, an ancient barrier dune running north–south through south Georgia and north Florida that acts as a natural sill of the eastern boundary of Okefenokee and Pinhook. (Both swamps may have derived from lagoons occurring on the landward side of a relict marine scarp.) Titanium ore produces a white pigment mostly used to replace lead in paints. It was being mined in Florida; Trail Ridge deposits were said to be the richest in North America.

The strip mine would operate twenty-four hours a day, seven days a week, for the next forty years. It would mean clear-cutting mile-square sections of Trail Ridge, building dikes to retain surface water, excavating to fifty feet with dredgers floating on twenty-acre ponds, and transporting about four hundred truckloads of ore weekly to Starke, Florida, for processing. The mining would require up to 750,000 gallons of groundwater a day.

DuPont insisted it could extract titanium without harm to the swamp. Hydrologists and ecologists insisted not. Secretary of the Interior Bruce Babbitt visited the refuge and publicly announced his opposition to the idea. People concerned about the swamp got organized. For eighteen months "stakeholders" battled DuPont Corporation. Gene Bernofsky, filmmaker, mine activist, and postal worker from Missoula, Montana, produced a twenty-minute documentary, "Trembling Waters," opposing DuPont's strip mine. Everywhere Gene has gone and made a documentary, the mine project has failed. Gene duplicated thousands of copies of the video and passed them out for free to anybody who'd take one. The videos circulated. Bruce Herbert, president of a Seattle-based investment firm, presented a resolution at the DuPont shareholders' annual meeting calling for a permanent stop to the mine. Although the resolution did not pass, it garnered sufficient support to be placed on the following year's ballot.

In one of the meetings of swamp defenders, in which Larry Thompson was present, some tired visionary, fed up with thinking reactively, said, "Whatever happened to the idea to join Okefenokee to Osceola National Forest?"

"I haven't heard much about that lately," somebody said.

"The Forest Service is lobbying for funding," somebody else said. "To little avail."

"Why not let's get behind that?"

Larry Thompson had helped form the Everglades Coalition in the early 1980s. This was a group of groups—local, state, and national—who knew that by working together they could accomplish more. Friends of the Everglades, the group begun by Marjory Stoneman Douglas, author of *River of Grass* and lifetime warrior for the 'Glades, became a member. The Everglades Coalition still meets regularly and is the mountain-moving force behind efforts to restore and protect the Everglades. Power lies in numbers.

Why not do the same for Pinhook?

"Great idea," someone said.

"Wonder what could we call it," one of Larry's friends mused. There were three important words: *Okefenokee, Pinhook, Osceola.*

OOP Coalition? POO?

I think David White, environmental attorney, gets credit for the name *POGO*. Pinhook Osceola Greater Okefenokee.

By the late 1960s two eminent American scientists, Edward O. Wilson and Robert McArthur, were looking at what they called island biogeography. Studying actual islands separated from continents at the end of the last Ice Age, they observed that isolation of habitat inevitably results in a loss of biota, or plant and animal species. The greatest losses occur on the smallest and most isolated islands; larger islands and those closer to mainlands have higher numbers of species.

Two decades later, ecologists began to apply the term island *to pockets of wild lands left in an increasingly fragmented landscape, and found the same results as Wilson and McArthur. Similar patterns of extinctions occur when species populations are hemmed in and cannot migrate elsewhere or replenish their numbers after disturbances like drought or fire.*

For many species, fragmentation of habitat, or home, leads to extinction.

You remember Pogo. He's the cartoon opossum thought up by Walt Kelly after a visit in the 1940s to Okefenokee. In 1943 Kelly created the comic *Bumbazine and Albert the Alligator*: "Once there was a big old alligator named Albert who loved chocolate cake." Bumbazine was a little boy who lived in Okefenokee Swamp with his pet alligator, Albert, but gradually Bumbazine faded and the comic centered on Pogo, a generous and modest opossum. About six hundred other identifiable creatures found voice in the cartoon, including Dr. Howland Owl, P. T. Bridgeport (a bear), Porky the porcupine, and Churchy-la-Femme, a turtle. They talked like this: "The natural born reason we didn't git no yew-ranium when we crosses the li'l yew tree and the gee-ranium is on account of cause we didn't have no *geiger* counter."

Kelly's characters often represented political figures. Simple J. McCarthy, a conniving bobcat, aped Senator Joseph McCarthy. His sidekick, Indian Charlie, represented Richard Nixon. J. Edgar Hoover was a bulldog and Spiro Agnew was a hyena in uniform. Their actions, expressions, and commentary, as political satire, struck deep.

Pogo started out slowly as a daily feature in 1949, was syndicated, and by the late 1950s almost six hundred newspapers subscribed to it. After Walt Kelly died in 1973, *Pogo* continued, managed by Kelly's family, in some form or another, until 1992.

Pogo the opossum uttered his most famous line upon seeing a garbage-littered swamp: "Yep, son, we have met the enemy and he is us."

Biologist Larry D. Harris, author of The Fragmented Forest, *proposed in the 1980s that fragmentation was the most serious threat to bio-*

logical diversity in the United States. Fragmentation alters the abundance and persistence of many species. Common species proliferate and rare species dwindle. This forever changes the definition of fauna, that incredible, irreplaceable biological heritage of a region.

Look at these examples: The passenger pigeon disappeared from the Southeast, but European pigeons are common. Snowy egrets are less common; cattle egrets are everywhere. Fire ants displace native species. Coyotes are colonizing the Southeast, but red wolves are not to be found. The English sparrow is ubiquitous, although the dusky seaside sparrow is gone.

Larry Thompson made a simple and courageous move. He invited everyone he could think of, especially those attached to an environmental group, to a meeting in Folkston, Georgia, in December 1997. Eight people came. From this meeting the POGO Coalition began. One of the first issues it would tackle was to squash the proposed mine, although its main mission would be to push for public purchase of lands sufficient to create a wild corridor stretching from Okefenokee to Osceola. As a group of groups, the new coalition could be more persuasive, more forceful, more powerful.

Stephen Williams of the Florida Panther Society attended the first meeting. "Together we can make the most impact in the shortest amount of time," he said.

Don Perkuchin, former refuge manager of Okefenokee Swamp, who, now free of the government, could work as an activist for ecological goals, agreed. "This is a fragmented ecosystem, and attempts to take care of its environmental concerns have been fragmented," he said.

"The POGO Coalition is going to be a force," said Linda Bremer of the Florida Sierra Club.

More organizations signed on: Florida Wildlife Federation, St. Johns Audubon, Apalachee Audubon, Florida
Defenders of the Environment, Georgia Sierra. Larry called
me and I joined. I was not representing an organization.

*As the amount of forest dwindles, species richness declines. Certain mam-
mals are more common in large forest tracts than smaller isolated patches.
The bigger the forest size, the more red squirrel, gray squirrel, raccoon,
and red fox. Wide-ranging mammals like panthers, black bears, mink, and
otters require large tracts of habitat in order to find prey, and adequate
cover or denning areas. Swallow-tailed kites, broad-winged hawks, barred
owls, pileated woodpeckers, and black-billed cuckoos need large forested
areas. Some songbirds, like worm-eating, hooded, and black-and-white
warblers, are generally absent in forest patches of fewer than fifty acres.*

*Fragmentation causes inbreeding among populations of animals,
including black bears.*

*Smaller habitats support fewer species. Small patches of wild habitat
most often get used by common permanent residents and by short-distance
migrants. Fragmentation is the primary reason for the decline of neotrop-
ical migrant birds. Endangered red-cockaded woodpeckers and scrub jays
will not traverse large areas of open or developed land in order to locate
suitable habitat.*

By March 1999 two major events had taken place. First,
DuPont signed a no-mining agreement with stakeholders,
which would halt the mine in exchange for ninety million
dollars—this covered permanent retirement of mineral
rights, purchase of the proposed mining site, creation of a
research center at Okefenokee National Wildlife Refuge,
and a handful of other endeavors aimed at enhancing rural

Charlton County, Georgia. The money, unfound as yet, was
to come from state, federal, and private sources.

The second event was that Congress appropriated one
million dollars to purchase another piece of Pinhook.

With so much success, and without the immediate
threat of mining or the desperate need to rally, POGO
Coalition's monthly meetings got harder to attend. People
turned to other projects. Larry left the Audubon Society,
which had supported his coalition efforts. And so the
POGO Coalition languished.

*Fragmentation produces more edges, which come with their own sorrows.
Excessive edges reduce populations of species dependent on large amounts
of forest interior. Some birds, such as the sharp-shinned hawk, Cooper's
hawk, hairy woodpecker, hermit thrush, veery, and many warblers, nest
only in interior forests. Populations of white-footed mice and chipmunks
decline in small "forest patches" to the point that they become locally extir-
pated. Often populations of species tolerant of edges and of habitat disturbance displace less common, less tolerant species. For example, red-bellied
woodpeckers have increased in abundance with rampant fragmentation,
colonizing territory that traditionally might have belonged to the endangered red-cockaded woodpeckers.*

*Species attempting to live along edges are subject to the dangers of
openness, including: 1) increased chances of nest predation by land or by
air, from crows, raccoons, cats, and dogs, 2) greater competition for nest
cavities (the red-bellied woodpecker vying for holes the eastern bluebird
might use, for example), 3) more nest parasitism, especially from the
thriving brown-headed cowbirds laying eggs in warbler nests (leaving the
hard work of chick raising to the smaller, less common birds), 4) higher
levels of parasites and diseases, including rabies and heartworms, and 5)
more death by poachers and glory-shooters.*

HUNDREDS OF SENSES

The world is too much with us; late and soon,
Getting and spending, we lay waste our powers:
Little we see in Nature that is ours . . .
—WILLIAM WORDSWORTH

FOLLOWING DIRECTIONS we've been given for a great walk into the middle of Pinhook, my husband and I reenter the swamp, this time on foot. Most of the roads reaching toward the heart of Pinhook are impassable. We drive in a mile or two on a stable, well-maintained road from the eastern boundary, and park. Carrying binoculars and camera and notepads, we take a tram heading west.

One of the great bodily functions we possess as mammals—as important as intellect, as crucial as movement, as vital as the heart pumping, pumping, or the liver filtering—is the enormous capacity of our senses. Wide-open they are, like flowers. Flower eyes. Flower mouth. The skin an enormous silky flower.

We have only one day for Pinhook, and I want to perceive as much as possible. I am present, tentacles out, ears perked, nose moist.

EYES: The eyes see the red-orange of tannic water seeping across the two-path tram. They see tangling expanses of saw palmetto, bay, fetterbush (March-blooming pink and white), and gallberry. Vines of catbrier. Cascading yellow jessamine, flowering furiously. Tracks of raccoon. The eyes watch for bears. Within a mile we count three piles of bear scat, stuffed with indicators of their carnivory—fur, crushed bones, and small claws, the largest of which is about one-half inch.

EARS: In the terrific silence that belongs only to nonindustrialized places, we hear, ahead of our passage, whirring wings of grasshoppers and soft plops of cooters plunging off logs into ditch water. We hear our own pant legs swishing together, and the low squelch of our rubber boots.

MOUTH: At first our tongues retain the residue of sharp cheddar cheese eaten in small chunks on blue-corn chips before we set out. Washed by the clean taste of our farm's well water. The dry grassiness of broom sedge swirling from mouthfuls of air.

SKIN: The sun burning our arms, which are tender from a winter mostly indoors and weeks of almost constant cloudiness. Wind against our necks. The cotton of long pants. An occasional mosquito, piercing.

Walking along, not hungry or anxious or tense or fearful, I suddenly smell an odor that reminds me of the muskiness of rattlesnake. Yet it isn't quite like snake. Sometimes plant odors resemble animal ones—like the weeds that when trampled replicate the stench of cat urine. For a few steps this bushy odor is real and distinct, a fecund smell of deterioration that is not death but fertility. A wan cloud of redolence.

"Do you smell that?" I ask my husband. I have a gut feeling. Hairs stand up on my arms.

"No," he says at first, but trusting me, stops. I back up a few paces, sniffing the air like an animal.

"Now I smell it," he says. "It's sort of like mothballs."

Could this be the odor of bear? We stand still, scanning the thickets around us, and listen. We smell again and again. We taste the air.

Only the motoring of dragonflies and the bright fluttering of tiger swallowtail butterflies interrupt the silent motionlessness of Pinhook Swamp. But some smaller sense, the one that prickles hairs on the backs of necks, that stirs like dislodged pebbles at the bases of brains, becomes known to us: in this case the sense of the presence of another animal, not our kind, and not very far away, protecting his or her own safety. What we smell we will never know. Species we know not. Big or small we know not. We walk on.

NOSE: Aroma of swamp. Sun-cured moss. Trickle of jasmine. Bear. Don't I wish the olfactory senses were sharper.

Wouldn't I wish all my senses to be keener?

Our senses function for safety and pleasure. They gather information that when fed to our brains drives most of our actions. Yet much of what we accomplish in our fervor to industrialize and technologize our world we do at the expense of arch sensual abilities. When we smoke cigarettes we dull our senses of smell and taste. Too long surrounded by the sameness of gray walls and square rooms, we dull our sense of sight, as well as our abilities to detect variations in patterns and colors and motions. With loud machinery, the firing of artillery, and high-decibel music, we impair our sense of hearing.

I am of course not forgetting the genetic or accidental losses of certain senses, which are beyond our abilities to heal. I am speaking here of preventable loss.

Ridding our environment of all potential dangers diminishes our need to hone our sensual detectors. Thus our capacities shrink. If we kill all diamondback rattlesnakes, we will never have to know what a rattler looks, smells, or sounds like. If we kill all alligators or red wolves, we will not have to recognize the signs of their presence. Most of what we have done to the land as agriculturists, as industrialists, as technologists, and as a people understandably terrified of harm diminishes the land, and thus diminishes ourselves. In this senselessness how will we recognize danger?

Nor do human sensual powers end with the primary senses. The sixth sense of intuition, along with, I believe, dozens of other senses, we have neglected. Sense of direction. Sense of longing. Sense of pitch. Sense of obligation. Sense of danger. Sense of being watched. Sense of another's presence. Sense of hostility. Sense of time. Sense of place. And so on. These are our evolutionary birthrights, and I believe we are losing them as we strive diligently to sanitize and safeguard and barricade our lives, so that we are never hungry or scared or drowning or eaten alive, or even bitten or stung, or sick. In doing so we become weaker creatures.

I am not interested in lost powers, but I am fascinated by a life that hones all human powers, even those we have almost lost completely. Especially those.

We know if it weren't for the road we wouldn't be here. There is such a tangle on the ground beyond the road. I cannot fathom what this place would have looked like had I seen it 150 years ago. The trees were taken. They have started to come back. Sunshine bathes everything, with water for miles below—a low sheet of running water, beautiful red organic water—and that middle space, to the height of a very tall human, is a tangle of thorny green. This is not the savanna of our early brain, birthplace of the human race, but a ragged labyrinth beyond our comprehension. Not what we evolved with.

Can't go over. Can't go under.

Got to go through.

Headlong is the way the bears travel, in tunnels plunged through the bristling shrubbery of titi and gallberry, where everything is set to prickle the tender human skin. Where there is not even a place to lie down. Yet we know animals live here, by the tracks of raccoons and piles of bear scat, and once the track of a bobcat on the tram, and turtles falling, falling. As if the sight of a human infuses them with terror, and they must dive into the oblivion of the tannic water.

We stay on the road. We turn right, then right again.

"Which way is south?"

"I don't know."

"Can you tell which way is east by the sun?"

"Behind us, I think."

After a long way, we turn right again.

"There's a Carolina wren."

"Not much birdlife."

"I like this candyweed."

"Are you scared out here?"

"No."

"Do you think this is the way back, all this turning?"

"I think so."

"We can always get back to the car. Turn around. Left, left, left."

"Is it A.M. or P.M.?"

"I can't tell."

Preserving the wilds of Pinhook means that perhaps we have learned something about moderation, that human vision may have been broader than we thought, that human genius considered the bounds, always, of our biological selves. So that the push toward a bionic man or woman, or toward robots or remote-controlled craft, was an attempt to escape the bounds of our biology, which is not possible. We accept the knowledge of our destructibility and the pain, both carnal and psychic, connected with that understanding.

With the saving of Pinhook, we are saying we are willing to accept our mortality, our humanness, our need to forage and feed and drink and breathe and shit. We are saying we are willing to accept the necessity of our sensuality.

"More is required of us than simply being swept along," Mahatma Gandhi said. Are we going to watch our culture and the world fracture and shatter? Or for the sake of the human being inside us all, capable of so much, are we going to stop the freight train of environmental destruction, much of it caused by corporate industrial globalization, and begin to remake the world? Are we going to begin to repair the damage?

FROG

THE TINIEST OF animals is enough for marvel. Staring into one of the puddles along the narrowest of tram roads, bordered by borrow ditches on either side overflowing with a liquid that some would not recognize as water, more like coffee diluted and cooled, Raven finds a frog. It is no more than a half inch long; even with legs extended it is barely an inch. It is colored a drab dark brown, except for the most brilliant markings of neon green along its back, a fluorescent V at the base of the head, and extending from the point of the V, a line dividing the frog in half. This is a cricket frog, which makes a sound like marbles clinking together. Spotting our towering visages, it pumps its fleshless legs furiously and dives across the puddle and into blades of broom sedge, a grass that colonizes disrupted areas. We cling to the vision of that mere fingerprint of a creature, a flicker of amphibious beauty, a morsel of imagination, because it signifies the presence of life.

Mostly Pinhook Swamp was divided from its own evolution, the slow unwinding of time, and forced to produce trees. For human consumption. This pocosin was enslaved then by timber companies, and by the needs and desires of humans. This was a long division: number of acres divided by what the pine trees were worth. An ecosystem divided by landowners. A forest divided by rows. Bear populations divided by highways. Water flow divided by ditches, made by borrowing dirt to built tram roads for hauling out the trees, which were divided trunks from roots.

The other part of the Pinhook's fragmentation was in our minds. We separated ourselves from it. We never heard of it. We never went there. We were ignorant or bored or frightened of it. And of a million other places much closer to us than Pinhook Swamp.

Let the land be reunited with what it was divided from. Let it be given back to itself, a captive let out of prison. Let it be given back to us.

The frog fascinates me. How it longs to hide. How it longs to save itself. How it understands nothing, I believe, of life beyond the puddle; we are monsters as seen from the shallows. The frog knows nothing of impinging danger bigger than this puddle, as its ancestors knew nothing of plans to drain the swamp to grow more trees, which would have made the place much less habitable for their kin. As biologist David Dorman said, "A pine plantation doesn't pose much of an obstacle to a bear that can travel 30 miles in a single night. But drain even 100 yards of swamp and you've thrown up a roadblock between populations of amphibians and invertebrates on either side." This frog would know nothing of talk that took place in dry meeting rooms far from this emptying cathedral. Although place-restricted, perhaps the frog knows everything it needs to know. How simple it is. How immersed. How present.

SILENCE

WALKING IN PINHOOK, I find the land uncommonly quiet. Something about the place's silence eats at me, until I want to ask, to find out, Why is it so quiet? I have not been able to figure out exactly what is missing. Of course the panther. The red wolf. The ivory-billed woodpecker. Swallow-tailed kites would have built homes in large trees that no longer exist.

Silence is frightening, because it is the sound of death, of annihilation. Silence is the ghost of the panther screaming like a woman in the flatwoods. Silence is the lostness of packs of red wolves. Silence is the vacuum of the whooping crane's heavy wings beating a meringue sky.

In silence anything is possible. In silence we die. In silence we lie in death. In silence we lie. In silence we re-create images of those things we have lost, until that memory is huge. In silence we lose that which means most to us. In silence life is snuffed.

Why is anything silent?

Out of contentment. Out of wisdom. Out of sleepiness. Out of fear. Because to be loud or even talkative would disrupt some ancient peace, perhaps the process of healing. Because water muffles.

How can the animals live with so much silence? Pinhook has a silence as powerful as all the silence in the world.

Sound is alive. Lively. Nonchalant. With sound we celebrate. Loudly we praise and are festive. Sound means life. The Carolina wren is alive and well, flittering into crevices of trees. We don't need to worry about Suwannee cooters, which satisfy us with their plops. Once in a while a carpenter frog pounds his tiny hammer in the sphagnum.

Pinhook, however, has always lived with this silence, except for the time it lived with the bulldozer building these tram roads, and with the saws, and with the trucks as they hauled away the once-living, bird-filled, sap-risen, green-leafed, satisfied, noise-making trees. Pinhook remembers the time before silence, before roads, before the modern age. It remembers trading with its neighbors to the south and to the north, and the east and the west. It remembers the recession of the Pleistocene Sea and what the sea left behind. It remembers what fires left behind, what storms left behind, what loggers left behind. It remembers the tambourines of leaves.

Silence always follows great calamities.

In Pinhook's memory the sound of humans is a calling to and fro on the watery, matted horizon.

So many of us are estranged from the land. We find its processes strange. We are afraid that nature equals death, and it does, but the other, more necessary truth is that nature means life.

For you, my beloved human, what does it mean to your life that the Pinhook has been saved, and that now we have preserved a state of wildness more than 750,000 acres in size, straddling two states?

Could it mean your life is enhanced? As are your children's? Could it mean your great-grandchildren may hear a red wolf calling or a panther cry?

Two great sounds denied to me.

RED WOLVES

THE LAST RED wolf was heard near Pinhook Swamp about 1915.

The end.

THE VISIONARY

ON A SWELTERING day in June 2004 I got to meet Larry Harris. Now professor emeritus of the University of Florida, he drove into Pinhook with an oxygen tank on the back of his pickup. He was rigged with clear tubes that traveled into his nostrils, held in place by an apparatus around the ears. When he alighted from the truck, he seemed much too healthy to be on oxygen—lean, with color in his face and the clearest blue eyes imaginable. He wore blue jeans and old boots.

Meeting Larry Harris was, for me, like making the acquaintance of Darwin. Both were scientists who had served humanity by figuring out something very important.

We were in Pinhook because of television. We'd been asked to be on a show called *The Natural South*, which was producing, at my urging, a thirty-minute segment on the Pinhook Corridor. We'd hook up with the show's crew, which predicted that we'd need to film all day, and also with a young biologist who studied bears, Jeremy Dixon of the Florida Fish and Wildlife Conservation Commission. So I had no time to do more than greet Larry, whose oxygen popped every few seconds, before we had to follow the television crew inland.

We were both riding on the back of the biologist's

agency pickup. I asked Larry how he came to understand Pinhook Swamp as a logical landscape linkage.

"I could see that our system of preservation didn't support native flora and fauna," he said. "Almost none of our eastern preserves are large enough to support populations of red-cockaded woodpeckers, for example. The obvious answer to the problem of decline and extinctions was connectivity. I was working in areas that were not big enough to support our native species. Because Pinhook is so wide, compared to its short length, it was a prime example. It could connect states, agencies, and natural areas."

The truck jostled and bounced through the rutted, poor roads of the pocosin. Larry clung to the wheel well and I sat in the truck bed, taking very messy notes. I had wanted to ask him these questions for a long time. He had been thinking about Pinhook when I was yet finishing college, before I realized my own power in the world, when I was more concerned about how to pay the rent or buy a new battery for my dilapidated car.

"How was your idea received?"

"Nobody had any heartburn at all signing on to this baby," he said. "It was even easy to persuade Ronald Reagan that we had to consolidate our land-preservation efforts."

I didn't have to prompt or question Larry much. He was eager to tell everything.

"We realized by putting tags on bears that they were moving between Georgia and Florida. We knew they needed linkages. The animals will show you what they need. I know a little something about landscape ecology, but I suppose they know more." He gripped the truck bed as we lurched over a particularly rough washout. "Remember when the collared panthers were released in Pinhook? They told us by their movements where they wanted to go. One went all the way to Augusta. They read something in the land that we don't."

"Is this corridor enough, then?"

"Oh, no. Where do we go from Okefenokee? How can we get hooked up to the Appalachian Trail? Then we can go all the way to Maine."

I understood that by *we* he meant wildness, he meant the constituents of wildness, he meant panthers and bears. And himself.

The crew stopped ahead of us, on a car-wide trail. Our vehicle stopped. We disembarked and squeezed past sweetbriar to get done the job that we had come to do.

For hours we filmed. The videographer lugged his big camera through the woods. The sound man walked, headphones clamped to his ears, his big furry microphone held up to the sky like a diviner's rod. We repeated ourselves over and over into the camera: "This is saw palmetto, a vital food for black bears and also useful to humans in the treatment of prostate problems." Or: "These are the tracks of bobcat." Over and over we strolled the same stretches of ground, walking slowly along the tram through the pocosin as the camera followed us, or ambling nonchalantly—over and over—along the water's edge. *Do that again. Say that again. Explain that.* Sometimes I strolled beside Larry, off into the pines, or moving from a distance back toward the camera, the elder scientist and his follower. Larry was able to leave behind his portable oxygen tank for short periods and I was alert for breathlessness or signs of fatigue in him. None came. Sometimes the crew filmed Larry showing me things, the difference between swamp titi and black titi, or upland blueberry.

But the repetition necessary for the filming wrought a

fierce boredom, and so our task soon lost any of its allure and excitement. How many times did I hear Larry identify wax myrtle or explain the value of alligators in a landscape? Too, the filming was more staged than we imagined: *Look out toward the sky, head tilted. More tilt. Take off the sunglasses; we started without them and we can't suddenly introduce sunglasses. Your hair is blowing in your face.* The sound had to be just right. None of the others could be talking. Even a small plane droning far off at the edge of the horizon halted the action and demanded repetition. Every few minutes a plane passed overhead. Sometimes one had not yet crossed before another entered the soundscape from a different direction. Later we would learn that airplanes were being rerouted because of the G8 heads of state meeting taking place a couple of hours away on the coast.

Then the crew wanted more. The landscape wasn't beautiful enough, interesting enough. *Is this all there is of Pinhook? Where is the wildlife? Where are the birds? Why is there so much planted pine? We thought it was a swamp. None of this looks like a swamp. Can you take us someplace else where Pinhook Swamp really is? Explain again why it doesn't look like a swamp.*

And nothing of Pinhook got any more exciting. I hoped for a line of wood storks or *wonking* baby alligators or bears, but all we had to show for the silence was the food the animals might eat and their tracks through the mud and sand.

The camera crew got hotter and hotter. Sweat trickled down their faces. They repeatedly wiped their brows and doused handkerchiefs with ice water to hang over the backs of their necks. All the ice water in the world couldn't cool them down now. Between shots they stood in the shade of trees, wondering what might rescue them from this godforsaken country.

We changed locations to a pine plantation. We found bear tracks on a remote road—the biologist could tell where the bear was coming from, where it was heading, and about how big it was. The crew got a little excited and filmed the tracks.

Anytime we could step away from the shooting, off into the brush, Larry and I talked. Even when the television producers were filming us, I was memorizing what Larry was saying, so I could get away from the camera, pull the folded ledger paper and pen from my pocket, and write down what he said. "The biggest cypress we know about is in central Florida," he said. "It's eighteen feet in diameter. We think it's the largest tree east of the Mississippi. But cypress get big as sequoia." Or he might start telling me how sphagnum is very acidic, and how where water leaves the Okefenokee the pH is 4, and at the Saint Marys it is 7, how every frog and amphibian has to search for the right pH. He said that these little animals have to go miles trying to find their natal ground. Or he'd talk about wildlife underpasses. But mainly we talked about Pinhook.

"Wild corridors maintain sheet flow, fire flow, predation, pollination, and seed dispersal, among other processes," he said. "I'm really really excited about this one."

By early afternoon the television crew said they'd had enough and they headed back to Atlanta. Larry went back to his home in Gainesville, the biologist went back to his desk, and we returned to the farm. After all of us were gone, the animals reemerged and began anew to lay their tracks on the ground.

SILAS MANN'S STORY

BACK WHEN I were a young man, I was in Pinhook a lot. This was in the '40s and '50s. There's some big islands back there, with beautiful pine timber on it. I'd ride my horse, saddlebags full of corn, back in there along the root road, to check on my hogs and my Cracker cows that ran wild. The road was called root because it was built out of whatever people could dig up. Nobody lived back there.

The timber company didn't care if people run their stock back in there. Back then the woods burnt and there was plenty of grass for the cows. The timber weren't hurt. The hogs ate that wampee root—they'd eat it and squeal. To humans it was hot and bitterish, but hogs were crazy for it. [The milky tubers of the water plantain, or wampee, were consumed by Native Americans, as well as by settlers.]

I went in sometimes and trapped razorback hogs. The company didn't care if you trapped hogs. We built trap pens out of cypress sapling poles. I'd tie an ear of shell corn to a string holding up a gate. When I come back and checked on my traps, there'd be a hog in there. Hogs gentled right up, feeding them corn. We could tell our animals apart because of the way we marked the ear.

Sometimes we'd have an old bear eating our calves and pigs. You get after them, they head for that swamp. You get in there, you in trouble. Mostly it's solid territory, but there's some deep holes. Mostly it's getting lost. People from outside have to holler you out.

Now, I wouldn't be able to go a hundred yards before I'd get turned around.

One night, my wife woke me up. "Silas," she said. "Something's messing with the hogs." An old bear had caught one of the hogs. He left with hog in his mouth. I watched him climb a four-foot fence—bobwire. He climbed the fence with hog in his mouth. Crazy me, I got out and woke up neighbors. We got the dogs on him. The dogs bayed up in Bert's Eddy Bay, but we couldn't get to him. I come in to home way after while, before day. I got a little drink of Hattie Call and got after that old bear again. Finally we found him up an old tree. We killed him at nine o'clock in the morning.

A widder woman lived near there and cooked us steak for breakfast. She taken charge of it. She fried up round steaks—that's the muscle on each side of the back. He was fat. We ate the steaks. They tasted good.

One time I went in Okefenokee with hog

dogs. They bayed up in a Bermuda patch and were making such a racket I had to kick my old horse in the side to get him up there. We got a little closer; I drew back the bushes. I was looking through palmetto fans. The dogs was fighting a cub bear. I was near Breakfast Branch and my gun was in the truck, a mile away. I thought I could take a pine pole to kill it. I knew its mama would kill me if she came back. I waded in, scared, and beat him to death. He never hollered. I put him over the horse and carried him home to dress out.

They'd put me in jail now. They protect them nasty things.

We ate 'em. They was meat for us.

We hunted gator back in Pinhook too, in the lakes. If you knew how to grunt like a baby gator you could call up a big gator. You would shoot him and get in there in the water and get him out, even if he sunk on you. A gator hide brung so much a foot. To cure it you put salt on it and rolled it up. A seven-foot gator brought $3.50. An acre of land was $3.00 to $3.50.

We'd go in Pinhook to hunt deer. We camped out. We trapped coons too and sold the skins. We tacked up the hides to cure. People would come by and buy them about twice a month. Roeann in Union City was a man with connections. He was the one bought mine for years.

I seen one panther in my life. One. Not a wildcat. We used to run wildcats with cat dogs— I'd get out of my good bed to do that. I mean I

seen a panther. That day I had been to Lake City
for brick. I was cutting across between here and
Lake City on an old dirt road, coming home, and
one jumped across the road. It was late afternoon and there was a big ole swamp on the
north side of the road. I'm sure that's where it
was headed.

We built us a log cabin. Me and my wife. She
got on one end of a crosscut saw and we cut
down the trees we needed. We'd drag the logs up
with a horse and peel them. The cabin was
twenty-four by thirty-four feet. We smoothed
cement with trowels in the cracks. We lived in it.
Those were some of the happiest days of my life.

I was young then and full of vinegar. I plowed a
mule, made corn and peanuts. I chipped boxes and
made turpentine. I sold raw gum to Jacksonville—
I'd carry three barrels in my pickup truck. The
plant was on the north side of town. I'd drive right
up to the plant and they'd unload it. I had my own
bees and would rob 'em. I had four or five colonies.
Garden stuff and fruit trees do better when you've
got bees.

My wife would go pick blueberries on the
edge of Pinhook. You couldn't hardly see her
eyes for the bushes. She'd put 'em in the freezer
to make pies. Blueberry pie. She could make a
good one. She'd pick those highbush blackber-
ries too.

She'd cook pies, chicken and rice, sour cream
cake, pound cake. She could do it all.

Her name was R. E. Maybe her folks meant

to name her Aury, but she went by the initials. She taught first at old Taylor School, and later at the high school on 122.

When she died I didn't even know how to turn on the old washing machine. She did all the washing, cooking, canning, ironing. She made me collect rainwater for her iron. Our well water here has iron in it that coats up on things. I'd fill quart bottles with rainwater. There's three settin' in there right now.

She's been dead two years next April. We were married sixty-seven years and nineteen days when she died. Not a day goes by I don't miss her. When R. E. died, it wasn't so much I lost my wife; I lost my best friend.

There's so many more people now. Ain't so many cows and hogs. There used to be a big ranch over here behind our place. Now it's just trailers. I used to know about new people moving in. I guess I don't circulate like I used to. Ever' Wednesday I go rake and clean off R. E.'s grave. The old cemetery is a-filling up. Soon we'll run out of land.

LOGGING

WE ARE WEST of Okefenokee, driving south on a two-path dirt road that we hope will be a shortcut to Pinhook. We have come through Fargo, Georgia, and crossed the Suwannee River very near its headwaters. The first spring wildflowers are still in the throes of ecstatic bloom.

The forest road leads through cutover pine plantations mostly belonging to the Langdale family, well known in these parts for landholdings. Through here all the forests are cut. There have been no houses for miles. In the middle of nowhere we come upon a dilapidated heart-pine homestead—a placard registers it as the Langdale homeplace, built 1891. We get out and pick our way past large, bushy cedars in what would have been the front yard, and carefully step into the unpainted gray timbers of the house. The porch slants downward, and pieces of its floor are missing. The doors are gone. In some places the floorboards have rotted through, and we walk carefully through the rooms, touching the fireplace bricks, the wood, the windowsills, watching for oak snakes, for mice. To stand this long, so isolated and neglected, this homestead had to be built with good wood. Even now its girders are strong, its foundations resinous and solid. The people who lived here have long ago entered graves dug for them. What a place they lived in. Think what they knew that we will never know. In this house I can feel a sense of place that I will never be able to have.

Outside the old house a tremendous, venerable live oak, thick with resurrection fern and Spanish moss, still grows. Some precious ounce of respect has saved it, for all around the forests are gone to tree farms. Maybe the Langdales loved this land, their home, but they cut it to hell and back.

They cut right up to the yard of the old house. Except for a few cedars and that big beautiful oak.

We pick our way back to the car.

How much land a species needs depends on the "home range" of that animal. Large animals have larger ranges. In most of the southern United States, because of fragmentation, only public land is large enough to support key species, including many that are imperiled or endangered, such as the red wolf and the Florida panther. The Southeast is being chopped into areas too small to support these civilizations.

Won't the same be true for humans? We don't really know how much habitat is required, or what the home range is for a human being. We know that fossil fuels have increased our ranging abilities. We "range," however, far beyond the territory required for our survival. In cities, in layers of apartments, many humans occupy the same thirty-by-thirty-foot area, a thousand square feet. And yet we know it takes a much larger parcel to meet a human's needs. Many back-to-the-landers have proposed getting by on five acres. I wonder how much wildness, by which I mean land in its natural state, is left per human. Need I say it? Surely we are already affecting our own rate of extinction.

Not far down the road we cross a wooden bridge over the Little Suwannee, whose water is pretty, almost orange. Soon after, halted by a locked gate, we must turn back, back to the highway. The way everybody else has to travel.

There's only one place a highway goes, and that's to a city. It leads in one direction only, and that is away from the wholeness that a native landscape offers, old trees dipping their limbs almost to the ground, hanging with epiphytic Spanish moss with its inconspicuous flowers, visited by pileated woodpeckers and brown-headed nuthatches. The city road never leads back to the country. The country road never leads back to the wild.

Turn right, turn left. Either way on a road you arrive at fragmentation.

On the highway all the way to Pinhook, five log trucks are the only vehicles we pass.

Connoisseur of Honey

WHO KNOWS MORE of a landscape than bees? They are within and without, above and below. A bee can travel great distances, as much as five miles, to forage on angiosperms, and then find its way back home. So it memorizes a landscape, and within its bee-goods it encodes that memory of place. Nectar, distilled, is the sweetest of a place's sweet. Honey is a delectable souvenir.

"Here's a place that sells honey," Raven says. He makes a U-turn and drives in. A man crossing between a modest country house and a big metal building notices us and waits.

Raven rolls down his window. "Can we buy honey from you?"

"How many gallons you need?" the man booms. He is in his sixties and large in every capacity—tall, strong, bearlike.

Raven glances at me and opts for caution. "Just a couple of pints."

My attention is torn between reading the man's face and watching a mist of mosquitoes float into the truck.

"I sell it by the barrel, all the way down to the half-pint," the man says. "Come on in. Let me show you." He leads us through a door, which we snap shut behind us, into an office decorated with bee kitsch among family snapshots, old bottles, and two computers, then across a bare concrete floor into a large room set up for bottling, which reeks of honey. In the middle of the room are two or three five-foot-diameter, stainless steel vats. The man lifts a metal flap lid on one. It holds a sticky pond of honey, enough to bathe in.

"You've got honey, all right," I say.

"We're a wholesale operation," the man says. "My daughter talked me into selling by the jar." He motions behind us. Wares line a wall—honey in plastic table-sized bears, jarred honeycombs, honey by the pint or quart. Tupelo, clover, gallberry, wildflower. "It was a good idea."

"Who buys honey by the barrel?" I ask.

"Oh, the people who make honey-nut cereal, honey candy, honey graham crackers . . ."

He explains to us the differences in varieties. For clover, he transports eighteen-wheeler loads of his bees to North Dakota, where, as they gather pollen on their legs, they pollinate crops. Wildflower is a little bit of everything local. This tupelo he's selling he didn't produce: Only the area around the Apalachicola River west of Tallahassee, Florida, grows enough tupelo to truly catch a flowering.

"All the gallberry honey made comes from this one area of south Georgia and north Florida," the man says. "It's concentrated in the Homerville area."

"Why's that?"

"Here's where it grows."

The true answer, I will later learn, is more likely "This is where it grows abundantly," because gallberry is a common evergreen shrub of the holly family found in coastal plains from Nova Scotia to south Florida, west to northeast Texas. Gallberry has two species here. Glabra (*Ilex glabra*) gets two to three meters tall and has bitter fruit—it will gall you. Coriacea (*Ilex coriacea*), which grows up to five meters tall, has sweet fruit. In the South gallberry blooms in the spring, small clusters of white flowers on short stalks. Although it survives in high pine forests, it loves wetter areas, of which there are plenty in this kingdom of flatness, like wet prairie savannas, bogs, seepage areas, and the lower slopes of wooded ravines.

So Pinhook Swamp is particularly suited to gallberry, and particularly rich in it. Of course the bees would go crazy for it, and stuff their honeycombed frames with its honey. The bears would go so wild for it they would have to be fenced from the hives with electrified wire.

"The timber people are ruining our gallberry," the beekeeper says. "I can't fault them for working hard and growing trees. But they have a detrimental effect on us honey producers."

"How?"

"Site preparation. The bedding and the bulldozing and the herbiciding kill the gallberry."

I take a jar labeled GALLBERRY from the shelf. The contents are a light amber with a yellowish tint.

This may be as close as I get to the center of Pinhook. Since I cannot communicate with the animals who have seen it for themselves and who have written entire books of their lives there, unreadable to me, and since I have not wings, I turn to bees. They fly, they crawl. They have sipped from the heart.

Raven is intrigued with the darker wildflower honey, thinking of the open white faces of dewberry blossoms, the small purple violets, I am sure, the tulips of the yellow poplar opening like cups high in the canopy, and all the diversity of lesser abundant flowers throughout the woods.

"Let's get one of each," Raven says.

The man's name is Mike. He came here years ago from Jacksonville, and only after he settled in this sparsely populated area of south Georgia did he find that his own grandfather had been born not ten miles away.

"Do you eat honey yourself?" I ask him.

He nods yes, after an almost imperceptible hesitation. Of course he has to eat honey, or say he does. "I put a spoonful in my coffee every morning."

"Can you tell the difference between their tastes?"

Again he says yes, although the hesitation is a split second longer. "I'm not a honey connoisseur," he says. "But I can tell the difference." He tells us about a very bitter honey he makes from blooming Brazilian pepper, the noxious exotic that threatens native ecosystems in peninsular Florida. This is a cheaper grade he sells to food manufacturing companies.

Warming to our curiosity, he shows us the entire operation, starting with an adjacent shed—a jumble of hives and supers, stackable wooden boxes in which bees carry on their operations. Mike demonstrates the machine that caps the wax combs, removing the lids of the tiny hexagons spilling with honey, and shows us the centrifugal extractor. Tubes run from the spinner to a huge vat where the honey is collected, from which it is strained into fifty-gallon barrels. Mike points out the collector that melts and forms the beeswax into golden bars. He shows us the frames that fit the hives, the wax sheets that fit the frames, the queen excluders. Steam-cleaning equipment. Then we're outside again. A truck loaded with boxes is ready to head to wherever there are flowers.

For some reason, probably because the past couple of days have become sunny and warm enough for a batch of insects to hatch, the mosquitoes outside are more horrendous than I have ever seen them, except for one encounter on Saint Vincent Island some years ago, during which a person couldn't stand still without thousands landing, proboscises ready, to suck her blood. It was a kind of torture. A person was torn between constant motion or constant pain. The honey yard was almost that bad: a murder of mosquitoes.

But the talk isn't over. We learn Mike's a bear hunter, or was until bear hunting was banned in Florida. Sometimes now he drives up to Georgia to hunt.

"How many have you killed in your life?"

He speculates, "Thirty or forty."

"For the meat?"

"I love it."

The three of us slap at mosquitoes constantly. The ones we miss fill with blood like hypodermic needles. I try to swat mosquitoes that Raven can't see on his shoulders and his forehead. This level of mosquito bite could send someone into anaphylactic shock.

"I'd better get on," Mike says. "I need to ride up and see about my bees. I'd be glad to show you the operation when it's in full swing. Just come back anytime."

With hearty good-byes and thank-yous, we dash to the truck and sit inside it a moment, sweating buckets, slapping mosquitoes that bumbled in when we did. We kill a bunch against the windshield, then head south on the deserted highway. When we roll down the windows, air blows the mosquitoes out and evaporates the perspiration on our necks.

Putting a landscape back together is a lot like doing a big jigsaw puzzle. Working a jigsaw puzzle, I start with the straight-edged pieces, so I get a frame first. For a landscape, you can't draw a big rectangle on a map and start filling it in. Restoration is more arbitrary. You start with what wild land you have. Then you look for spare pieces scattered about that match what you already have. If one fits, you plug it in, and then find another with the same thread of stream, and another. Breakfast Branch. Run Swamp. Moorehead Bay. Moccasin Swamp. Middle Prong of the Saint Marys River. Until you begin to see the shapes of the missing pieces, and you search for those shapes.

The more pieces in a puzzle, the more fragmented a place, and the harder to put it back together. In the case of Pinhook, the pieces were large and there weren't many of them, so the puzzle has been relatively easy, an intermediate puzzle. Easier, say, than reconstructing the tropical hammock that was the Florida Keys.

You connect one axis until you build a wildland bridge. You close a gap. Then you fill in the rest of the frame. Piece by piece, the puzzle is assembled, reassembled, until it forms a picture.

Later, other pieces you didn't even remember were missing will come. Naturally. The trees every year grow taller and wider. The roads heal over. Ditches erode and fill. Fire returns. More land gets added along the sides, buffers and wild land and corridor. Songbirds rebound. Black bears reterritorialize.

The picture grows more beautiful.

BLACK BEARS

BLACK BEARS ONCE occurred throughout the Southeast, but are now relegated to scattered populations. In Florida, for example, where bears are listed as a threatened species, there were, historically, eleven thousand bears. In the late 1990s bear populations in Florida were figured at between one thousand and fifteen hundred. This dispossession is due to loss of prime bear habitats and vegetated travel corridors between habitats. Bears prefer forested swamps with dense understory vegetation, as well as pine flatwoods and sand pine scrub. Pinhook, then, is perfect.

Black bears require large home ranges: males up to seventy square miles, and females about ten. About a hundred thousand acres of bottomlands are needed to support a population of between fifty and two hundred bears, depending on the quality of the habitat. To support a thousand bears, anywhere between three and a half and four million acres are needed. This could include agricultural land, as long as there is escape cover near the fields.

Besides loss of habitat, road mortality is the greatest threat to wild black-bear societies. Between 1976 and 1996 Florida roadkills steadily increased, with less than five in 1976 and more than sixty in 1996. Seventy-five bears were killed on Florida roads in 1997. In one year, seventy-five bears.

Road mortality in Osceola National Forest is low: one bear every couple of years. In the twenty-year period between 1976 and 1996, twelve bears were killed on roads in the counties that make up Osceola—the fewest of any population in the state, probably because of the remoteness of the area. According to one local account, unconfirmed, five bears were killed on Highway 2 in the five-month period following November 2002. One per month.

Twice as many bear are killed on roads in fall (October through December) as any other season. They are moving to avoid hunters, to disperse (juveniles), and to search for food in preparation for winter—because of mast availability, bears forage predominantly in the uplands in summer and fall, but relocate into the bottomlands in winter.

Day-to-day movement has always been necessary for all foraging organisms, including humans. Unlike clams or oysters, we don't live in flowing water that will bring our nutrients to us. Nor do many thousands of species. Even plants move their roots in a search for water, and their leaves in a search for light. In fact, a species' ability to move in large degree determines the fitness of that species to survive. Animals move in order to forage for food and other nutrients, find water or shelter, utilize seasonal environments (elk move down out of the mountains in the winter). Sometimes animals move to accommodate life stages, as the flatwoods salamander migrates to lowlands for breeding, and some species migrate to return to birthplaces. On a grander scale, species move to expand their ranges, colonize new environments, sometimes to new continents, and to adjust to climate change. Fragmentation represses movement. In fragmentation, movement may mean death.

Sow bears breed from May to July, for the first time at age three and a half. Black bears tend to give birth every other year, usually two cubs born in January or February. Cubs stay with their mothers for about eighteen months. Longevity is up to twenty-five years in the wild. Full-grown black bears weigh between 150 and 600 pounds. (They can get bigger—a 624-pound bear was hit and killed on a Collier County highway in 1968.)

Usually solitary, bears roam during the day except in well-peopled areas, where they will become nocturnal. Bears are very sensitive to human disturbance, and may quit an area simply because of the presence of trails. Narrow and infrequently traveled roads may be used by bears for movement and for foraging. They have a great sense of smell, good hearing, and can see colors. They are not normally aggressive—there are only fifty-two documented black-bear attacks in the past hundred years in this country.

Bear diet in the Southeast has been scrutinized painstakingly. From 1995 to 1999 biologists who study the animals briefly captured 209 bears on 351 occasions in the Pinhook wildland corridor; they noted if the bears were captured in Georgia or in Florida. The biologists analyzed more than twenty-one hundred bear scats and examined the stomach contents of those captured. In fall they found that the mainstay of bear diet throughout Pinhook Swamp was saw palmetto berries, along with black gum fruit, with small amounts of palm shoots, gallberry, and grasses thrown in. The difference between Florida and Georgia bears became evident in the study of their summer diets. The summer menu of Georgia bears was mostly huckleberry, blueberry, and grasses. Thirty-five percent of what the

Florida bears ate was corn—regular old shelled corn. They were being fed. And by whom? Hunters.

Gallberry, blueberry, saw palmetto shoots, and wild grape accounted for the rest of the summer diet of Florida bears, with trace amounts of greenbriar, sphagnum, and grasses.

Animal matter in all the bears' stomachs, at all times of year, was negligible, and included beetles, ants, and turtles.

Bear hunting was outlawed in Florida in 1993. Why, then, would the hunters feed the wild animals? Maybe the answer lies in the fact that the tradition of bear hunting continues in south Georgia, in the environs of the Pinhook system, three weekends, or six days, each fall, and often the old-time Florida hunters come north to participate in Georgia's hunts. Perhaps the shelled corn is their contribution. In 1999 the total number of bears killed by hunters in Georgia was forty-eight, twenty-nine with the aid of bear hounds and nineteen by still hunters.

How do hunters access the bears? By roads. The greater the occurrence of roads, the greater the hunting pressure on bears.

I have accompanied south Georgia hunters on a bear hunt; some of the bear hunters are friends of mine. They are respectful of the animals and devoted to their place, and I enjoyed my time with them. But never could I overcome the feeling that bear hunting, though a worthy tradition, was wrong. With bear populations diminished and bears limited to pockets of vestigial wildness, how could we chase them, shoot them, and eat them? Maybe one day, but now? How can we fail to admit that techno-industrialization has made the tradition of bear hunting impractical, thus obsolete?

ROADS

HOW CAN I hate roads? They are the way we pass through this world, the way we visit each other, the way we connect places. They are the formula by which my beloved comes home to me. They are the romantic vias to other lives, other possibilities. They are the way we enter the world of humans.

In 1979 C. R. Ferris determined that in Maine each kilometer of I-95 built displaced 130 pairs of breeding birds, which translated into 62,400 pairs of breeding birds along the 480 kilometers of I-95 in the state. For a roadway that is 30 meters wide, each kilometer of length deletes 750 acres of active or potential wildlife habitat.

A 1983 study found that 6.3 million kilometers of roadway took up 20 million acres in land surface across the United States, an amount that equals the combined area of all our national parks.

In the natural history of roads, human passages evolved from path to trail to trace to way to lane to road, but at some point the meaning of the word *road* changed. As long as humans perambulated, we had no need for a thoroughfare wider than our swinging arms. As long as we drove horses, we had no need for roads wider than a team, with maybe, in populated areas, a lane for wagons to pass. Roads connected people to each other, threads through wilderness.

Road once was a verb meaning "to join"; now it connotes "divide." In our past one hundred years of life in this country, since the Model T was created in 1908 following the invention of the automobile in Europe, our roads have ever widened, until they became great swaths gouging through the landscapes. The widest road I have ever seen was in Los Angeles, about 24 eighteen-wheeler-width paths, half going one way and half the other. Dividing everybody from everybody. Each person in his or her own car, divided.

Roads may bisect home ranges established by wide-ranging mammals or birds, territories that we cannot see with our eyes the way we can see picket fences and NO TRESPASSING *signs, and sometimes roads divide natural migration routes. It is along roadways that exotic, often invasive, species get introduced and spread.*

Roads are sometimes useful to animals. Roads may offer the opportunity for unhindered movement, as with panthers and bears in the Everglades, and often roadways provide new food sources, such as spilled grain, food thrown out car windows, and carrion. Bald eagles, for example, are seen dining on roadkill (which makes them more vulnerable to accidents). In some cases the roadways provide new habitat, especially for species such as the gopher tortoise that need clearings.

We mistakenly think that four-lane roads into rural areas will bring prosperity and development. We build interstates and parkways that allow fast travel, such as the road that quickly brings Atlantans to coastal Georgia, Highway 441, and these roads bypass the rural towns that have survived in part because of the business of passers-through. These new roads are not moderate in size and structure. On the contrary. New roads being built in Georgia, as previous governor Roy Barnes explained, "to bring a four-lane within twenty miles of any Georgian" are violently immoderate. But a four-lane interstate highway, being wider and paved, has greater effect on a landscape than a two-path road.

New highways everywhere (check out Mississippi) are unnecessarily destructive to life. In the worst-built roads, two directions of traffic are separated by a wide, ecological dead zone of median, mostly free of trees in case of accidents, and the shoulders of the road are at least a hundred feet wide, planted with high-maintenance grass. These roadways cut a swath one-eighth of a mile wide through the countryside.

Loss of land is a passive form of fragmentation. The automobiles that accompany the roads are active fragmentation. In 1974 more than 146,000 deer were killed on U.S. highways. Highway collisions accounted for 45 percent of all known panther deaths in the 1980s. In a 2.9-mile section of highway crossing Paynes Prairie, a state preserve in Alachua County, Florida, 13,000 snakes were counted dead from highway collisions, in a study that lasted four and a half years. The reptiles, which totaled about 1.3 tons, were killed crossing the portion of Highway 441 that bisects the preserve, or while sunning on the pavement. On a single day—February 22, 2000—90 roadkilled turtles were collected on a one-third-mile section of U.S. Highway 27 in Leon County, Florida, by biologist Matthew Aresco of Florida State University. The road bisects Lake Jackson. In England a 1987 study by the Fauna and Flora Preservation Society found that British drivers kill more than 20 tons of toads per year. A 1980 study in the Netherlands discovered that over 800,000 birds and mammals are killed per year on Dutch highways.

In addition, automobile emissions ranging from heavy metals such as lead to monoxide-laden exhaust fumes contaminate the rights-of-way. One scientist, P. F. Scanlon, studied small mammals next to highways and learned that they carry greater concentrations of heavy metals than small mammals found elsewhere. In addition, chemical herbicides are commonly used to maintain rights-of-way, and these impact not only inhabitants of the roadways, but the animals that prey on them.

In many cases four-lanes (like Wal-Marts and other chain stores) are built where they are not wanted or needed. Even if needed, a four-lane highway can minimize its impact on wildness and vital environmental processes.

I have become increasingly bitter about the ignorance of the federal Department of Transportation, state road departments, and county road supervisors. I am convinced that a road-building lobby as organized and destructive as the development lobby is driving new road-building projects. Many roads are wasteful. Many are unnecessary. Dare me to say it—*all* are contrary to environmental ethics, and *all* are enemies of wild America.

Wildlife underpasses are another kind of corridor. Wildlife agencies are experimenting with wildlife crossings in Lake and Collier counties in southern Florida, where bears are especially hard-hit. A guidewall and culvert system at Paynes Prairie, Florida reduced mortality of fauna by 64 percent (excluding birds and tree frogs, the ecopassage reduced wildlife mortality by 93 percent). At Lake Jackson, a temporary fence that guided reptiles toward culverts has helped reduce wildlife carnage until a permanent ecopassage can be built. These crossings are expensive, particularly when roads must be retrofit, but are being used by a menagerie of wildlife, with varying and often great degrees of success.

Panther Reintroduction

DURING THE SETTLEMENT by white people of this country, our megafauna managed to survive a massive campaign to exterminate them. Now we are desperate, in our present state of development, to keep from losing the last of them. The Florida panther, for one, is on the brink of extinction. America is down to fifty or so of these big cats, roaming the extreme south of Florida, mostly the Everglades and Big Cypress Swamp. In 1967 the Department of the Interior listed the panther as endangered, and in 1981 Florida passed the Florida Panther Recovery Plan, a last-ditch outline for saving the species. Scientists identify loss of habitat as the major threat and reason for the panther's downfall, and admit that because of a shrinking prey base in south Florida, recovery of the species will not be possible without reintroduction of panthers elsewhere. The panther won't be recovered until at least five hundred adult panthers exist in three or more independent populations.

Therefore in 1993 biologists released nineteen mountain lions, also called cougars (the Florida panther is a subspecies), on the western edge of Pinhook Swamp. They wanted to determine if the sparsely populated wild lands of northern Florida and southern Georgia might sustain the native cat, and they also needed to study social structures of introduced animals. Of the released cougars, some were raised in captivity, some were captured wild in Texas, and some had been captured wild and held in captivity for a time. Eleven were female, eight were vasectomized males; all wore radio collars. The animals would be recaptured once the study was complete.

Scientists tracked the mountain lions for more than two years, from February 22, 1993, the date of the first release, until June 30, 1995, when the last animal was recaptured. Fifteen of the cougars claimed home ranges. They clung to forested wetlands and pine forests, and dramatically avoided fields, urban land, and open water.

The panthers were not supposed to reproduce. But in July 1993, believe it or not, one of the female panthers, T39, began to exhibit what the biologists, who were radiotracking her movements, defined as denning behavior; her movements became confined to a small area. Yep. On August 4 she was seen with a kitten, which biologists located and attempted to capture alive. The kitten died as a result of being hit with a tranquilizer dart.

Later, females T31 and T32 exhibited denning behavior, but were never observed with kittens. In February 1995 a kitten was killed on Highway 441; hunters who saw the mother reported she'd had a second kitten with her. Blood samples from the kittens concluded that male T33 could "not be excluded" as the father.

One or more of the vasectomies had failed.

When residents of the Pinhook area became aware of the study, some began to fret. Maybe some panicked. Petitions circulated that opposed the reintroduction, asking that the cats be removed. More than six hundred people signed the petitions; half as many showed up at a rally in opposition. Government agencies backpedaled; because of fierce local opposition, and without a clear plan for the next step in bringing back the panther, the cougars were recaptured.

Seven of the lions, including two of the surprise young, had died during the study. Two were illegally shot, three were killed by vehicles, and two died during capture. One kitten was recaptured because she wouldn't follow her mother.

Meanwhile surveys showed that a swelling majority of Floridians supported reintroduction. In 1998 Stephen Williams, founder of the Florida Panther Society and a man passionate about wildness, walked 125 miles in ten days from the Osceola National Forest to the Florida capitol in Tallahassee to deliver a petition to the governor, House, and Senate, asking that the reintroduction efforts continue. There was no response.

The countdown of the Florida panther toward extinction continues.

To reintroduce the panther is to reintroduce a giant fear of the wild, and also a giant wonder. It is not our duty to ask which is greater. To have the animal is always greater.

But the landscape the panther first knew is not the present landscape, so unless its ranging acreage is large enough, we have condemned the animal to the fate of living in a zoo. With Pinhook, we are not trying to create a zoological park, where we can gaze at rare animals up close. We are trying to create a place that mimics as closely as possible a natural order. This Pinhook Swamp is a piece of the world we have not stepped too hard on. It holds black bears yet, and sandhill cranes and bobcats. Getting panthers back wouldn't be impossible. Somewhere in its bosom the land aches for its creatures to be returned.

One afternoon in Alaska I witnessed the release of a bald eagle. A juvenile, it had not developed the white head and tail of adults, so was dark brown with white splotches. The eagle waited in a carrying cage draped with a towel, under a hemlock, while a small congregation gathered on a bridge overlooking an inlet of Sitka Sound. Far out in the water buffleheads and Barrow's goldeneyes by the hundreds floated.

We were on the hundred-mile-long island of Baranof, named for a Russian governor in Sitka, the largest of the island's three towns. The beautiful landscape of Alaska could make one complacent. Sitka backs up to the rugged, snow-covered peaks of the interior of Baranof Island, where the population of grizzly bears is estimated to be one per square mile. In the center of Sitka, in Totem Park, there are a few old-growth hemlock trees, and only a short distance from town, a matter of a few miles, grow groves of virgin Sitka spruce, hemlock, and cedar.

As a chick this eagle had fallen from its nest near Ketchikan. Its parents were not caring for it where it huddled down on the unforgiving rocks, and when rehabilitators attempted to replace it in its nest, they found the large snag shaky. They were afraid the whole business would come crashing down.

The chick arrived at the veterinarian's at the Alaska Raptor Center. It was still covered in charcoal-colored down, although it was almost full size. (Eaglets reach full size quickly, in about eleven weeks.) Thereafter when the vet cared for it, he wore a white sheet made into a robe and a large eagle mask. "There's no fooling a chick," he told me. "It didn't for a minute think I'm an eagle. It just didn't know *what* I was." For the last two months of its captivity the eagle was sent to Washington State, to a bird rehabilitation center where it learned to fly. Because the center's flight way was only two hundred feet long, the eagle never once soared. Now it was home again in Alaska and ready to be released.

The event happened quickly. A woman from the raptor center spoke a few words. Then a businessman who had provided chickens to feed the bird and who was invited to do the honors leaned across the side of the cage and freed a spring-lock door. The eagle never saw the man's face. It bounded through the opening into an overcast day, and for a full minute crouched, dazed, on the pebbly beach, gazing around. Suddenly it beat its great wings and took to the air, flying as it had done over and over in the flight way. At two hundred feet no mesh stopped it. This was the eagle's first flight into real, open sky. Solo. It flapped, strong-winged, and wheeled out over the glittering bay, then rose higher and higher until it joined a fellow eagle in the thermals. Two brown crosses soared above a line of people who watched, hungry for miracles and signs of hope, on a bridge above a rocky beach.

That evening out of the blue, Raven said, "Tonight there is another bald eagle free in the world."

We gather eggs. We baste to gather a skirt's waistline. We gather round. Families and neighborhoods gather together. We collect birds fallen from nests. We gather information. We pile money. We collect bric-a-brac, usually of like nature to display together. We gather cotton to make bales of it. We gather peas and beans and okra, more gathering up of smaller amounts to make a larger amount. We collect drops of rainwater into buckets to water our gardens. We call our children home.

These are addition and multiplication.

There are as many examples, and maybe more, of subtracting and dividing. Breaking down. Most of them are less happy. Dispersal of a family. Fading of a petroglyph. Erosion of soil. A throwing away. The wind blows away a sheaf of papers. Chickens scatter. Someone gets poorer. Exile of a people. The draining of resources. Attack.

In the math of nature, subdivisions are the wrong answer.

"By doubling the size of Osceola and connecting it to Okefenokee, we will come a long way in bringing back the panther," Larry had said to me. "We will be saving the face and the character of America. We can bring the panther back if we haven't built shopping malls and five-acre ranchettes on their land."

Ecologists now recognize that ecological restoration must be based on rewilding, a concept that recognizes the necessity for large carnivores. To flourish, those predators need core, mostly roadless areas, as well as habitat connections between those areas.

We could celebrate the return of panthers: Pinhook Homecoming. Welcome home, panthers. A release party.

How they too would celebrate.

WATER

THE RESOURCE THAT people are most worried about is water. "You know how to make an instant environmentalist?" Larry asks me.

"No." I know it is a joke.

"Just add water."

The Pinhook Corridor supplies millions of people, mostly Floridians—some of whom already experience saltwater intrusion into the aquifer—with drinking water.

Two great rivers, the Suwannee and the Saint Marys, rise from Okefenokee and drink from Pinhook Swamp and bear their precious burdens southward. The invisible divide between the two river basins is often hard to figure. Area rainfall determines the direction water flows— whether Pinhook gives or receives water from Okefenokee, and which river receives water from the swamp. Between 53 and 58 inches of rain fall annually.

The headwaters of other black-water streams, like Little Suwannee Creek, Moccasin Creek, Gum Creek, and Little River, arise in Pinhook, joining the Suwanee or the Saint Marys in their journeys to sea.

Like the animals, water in Pogo's Corridor both slumbers and *moves*. This means that water finds rest in the prairies, sloughs, and lakes, and like migrating hawks, it passes through. Part of saving Pinhook means restoring the movement of water, so that it remains a sheet. As Florida biologist David Dorman has said, "A hundred years from now, you're going to be able to drop a minnow at the top of the Okefenokee Swamp [sixty miles north] and see it swim all the way to me and keep on going."

NIGHT

NOT LONG AFTER, and still before dark, we turn east into the national forest and drive about ten miles of rutted, rain-pooled roads to a Forest Service campground underneath a fire tower. The tower is fenced off and locked, or we would climb it. Three families of campers are here. We pull into the corner of the campground, as far from the night lamp as possible, and first thing, we dig out these fancy shirts we bought for the trip to Alaska, in preparation for biting insects. But how could Alaska produce anything more vicious than the bombardments of mosquitoes in the wet pinewoods of southern Georgia? The shirts are sewn of white cotton, with a panel of netting under the arms and down the sides. Each has a hood, with a visor of black mesh that zips up over the face. We cozy up into our antibug shirts and listen as relentless mosquitoes bomb us. It's great to be unreachable.

"What do these bug people expect us to do with our hands?"

"Gloves?"

"It's so hot."

"Maybe longer sleeves?"

"Maybe. At least you can wear the shirts with nothing underneath."

We set up camp—tarp, tent, pads, sleeping bags. Then we lower the tailgate and bring out homemade scones.

"Let's have a little bread on our honey," Raven says. I open the gallberry, and he the wildflower, and we learn a second flaw of the antibug shirts—there's no zipper for the mouth. You have to unzip the entire face visor to eat. Bugs are soon up our noses, around our eyes, biting our temples, while we scarf biscuits drowned in honey.

This is the flavor of Pinhook Swamp—wild yet demure, strong yet delicate, exotic yet plain. Homespun. The dripping, sticky, sweet, golden Pinhook Swamp—not the taste of it but the swamp itself—all over our mouths and hands. All over our faces and necks from mosquito slapping. A kind of holy communion. Honey communion.

Luckily the campground has a spigot.

Later by night cloud Raven prepares to cook venison that has been marinating all day in the cooler, and to steam new potatoes. He has bad news. "I forgot to bring matches." The venison is ready, the stove assembled and primed, the potatoes scrubbed and in a pot.

I didn't bring matches either.

I search the bag that held the stove, then my day pack (coins, pens, emery board), then the glove compartment (broken sunglasses, individual ketchup packets). How to get fire, the most basic element of human survival, source of warmth, purifier of water, transformer of food?

One of us remembers the truck's cigarette lighter, but have no idea if it works. Raven pushes it in. It doesn't. Maybe the engine needs to be switched on. A rainstorm moves in above us. The venison collects bacteria.

"This lighter should work," Raven says, emphasizing the *should*. He turns the key again. This time when he relieves pressure the lighter pops out, glowing red. Previous campers left us the gift of a few six-inch lengths of fat lighterd on the picnic table, and I peel off a splinter. Surely the wood, so packed with resin, will burst into flames when held against glowing metal.

The wood smokes and singes until the lighter fades to cool.

"Let's try paper," Raven says. More smoke and mirrors.

For these few minutes we reverse the evolution of human tool using, which has gone from fire to machine. Finally Raven cradles the lighter and lays the slightest edge of tissue against it, blowing gently. The single flame flares and catches. Fire is so instantly powerful. It's like a pygmy rattler materialized in your hands, growing fanatically to dragon. It can turn you to ashes. Raven dashes toward the stove with his handful of flames. Ours is the variety of camp stove that utilizes a collar filled with fuel that heats a brass chamber, building pressure until the burner is able to suck enough fuel out of the bottle to light. Fuel has spilled on the picnic table. When the stove lights, the table lights. Now we have a flaming picnic table, its brown paint readying to bubble. We stomp the fire out and Raven soon has the pans spitting and singing.

We eat to the music of the first chuck-will's-widow, southern brother to whip-poor-will, calling from the woods on its way north, where for many miles before it there will be blessed wildness.

The biggest question is, How do we surround ourselves with wholeness, how do we put our lives back together? I have a few answers, but it's a question we each have to ask ourselves. Think: What does wholeness mean to me? What would a life of wholeness look like? What could I do to make my life more functional and more fun?

This is the most urgent business we face in the twenty-first century, this question: How, in all this fragmentation, can we lead lives of wholeness?

By taking the word estranged *out of our personal dictionaries.*

By rejoining ourselves to others (in numbers the human psyche can comprehend).

By saving large tracts of land for wildness.

By restoring large blocks of land to wildness.

By returning ourselves to wildness: relearning.

In the middle of the night a terrific thunderstorm wakes us. Lightning jabs like devil's forks all around, and rain pelts the tent. It's an old canvas in need of weatherproofing, and so it leaks from all directions. Most of the rain weeps down the sides of the tent before dripping in. The ground cannot absorb the onslaught of water. The slash pine beside which we are sleeping shielded us from the light, but it's the tallest tree around, a lightning rod. We worry. We huddle in our sleeping bags atop their pads, as if lying on two rafts, and manage to stay dry. Everything else in the tent is wet. Everything.

Meeting Johnny

AFTER WE LEAVE Will and Larry, with well-wishes and hugs, at the Forest Service that first visit, we drive back to Lake City. It is now 2 P.M. and we have eaten neither a proper breakfast nor dinner (as we call it). In the apple aisle of the supermarket, a man comes up and grabs me. It is Johnny Dame.

"Johnny! This is unbelievable!" I say, hugging him.

"It's getting spooky," he says.

"How did you find us?"

"I saw a truck in the parking lot with Georgia license plates and a lot of bumper stickers. I wondered if it could be you." Johnny lives life in an ardent way. When he talks he gets very animated and makes enthusiastic hand gestures to illustrate his points.

"What in the world are you doing here?"

"I've been in Lake City meeting with a librarian friend of mine. She's been helping me research this latest art piece. It's a flag, a big flag, big enough for the side of a building. Each state is going to be represented by an endangered species. I've been looking up the species to use."

We met Johnny Dame the weekend that Raven and I met, on the main street of White Springs, Florida, an hour away. Johnny was finishing a mural he was painting on the outside front of Suwannee Cafe. He invited us inside to see the mural in the dining area. On three walls he'd depicted the local landscape, plentiful with native flora and fauna, through four seasons and twenty-four hours of day: a labor of genius and love. Johnny is native to a small town in central Florida, son of a politician. He is a naturalist; a man of vision; a believer in a world more imaginative, more peaceful, more habitable, and more sustainable than the one that corporations have created. The card he handed us had no address, only a name and telephone number.

That afternoon, because we loved his mural so much, we visited River Gallery, the front rooms of Stephen Williams's home on the Suwannee River, dedicated to wildlife art. Johnny Dame's paintings were prominent.

The painting of Johnny's that struck me dumb and sent me into tears was a bird's-view depiction of the Suwannee River basin. The perspective was from far enough in space that one could see the curve of the earth, yet close enough to distinguish leafy mounds of individual treetops. Below the screen of green tree canopy, one saw no trappings of human life—no highways, no cars, no houses, no lights, no power lines. Just the wild earth. The river threaded through, pouring out of Okefenokee and Pinhook. Ichetucknee Springs bubbled up into floodplain forest. Way up toward the top of the painting, just where the earth curved in upon itself and the eye could see no farther, lay my home in south Georgia.

The painting was the earth made whole. It was our bioregion, replete with the glory of its full biology. Here was life resplendent, our natural home.

After our first meeting, it was uncanny how often we

ran into Johnny Dame—at the gallery again, at the folk festival two months later in White Springs, at a farmer's
market in Gainesville. I wanted Johnny to come paint the
Altamaha River. He could stay at our house, I told him.

"Yeah!" Johnny said. "I'd like to do that. I'll get up there
one day." Johnny was a man of the moment, a deeply
thoughtful, caring drifter on the winds of life.

Near dusk one evening during the 2004 Florida Folk
Festival, Raven and I were swimming in the smooth, tannic,
dark-amber water of the Suwannee River when we noticed
a familiar figure strolling down the riverbank toward us.

"Is that Johnny Dame?" I asked Raven.

He squinted. "That looks like him."

As the man approached, we identified Johnny with cer-
tainty and called out his name.

"Heavens!" Johnny exclaimed. "This is too uncanny. I
saw a couple swimming but in the dimness I didn't recognize you." He waded toward us. "How are you?"

In late May the grand river is temperate, cooler than the
air temperatures, and very soothing. It is shallow from lack
of rain. We were on our knees in the fine sand, water to our
necks. We told Johnny we were doing great.

As darkness came upon us, as we soaked in the great
luxury of the wild and beautiful Suwannee—composed as it
is of waters from Okefenokee and Pinhook, colored by
their ancient cypress, and informed by the splashing of alligators and otters and bream—Johnny told us that he judges
the success of his life by how many nights he spends out of
doors.

He started counting in 1996. That year, he slept 39
nights outdoors, in a sleeping bag on the ground or in a
tent. At the end of 1997, he remained again at 39 nights

outside walls. Then in 1998, the figure rose to 78, and in 1999, 99.

During 2000 and 2001, because of circumstances of work, the number of nights Johnny camped dwindled, 25 to 30 each year. But in 2002, Johnny was back to living a bohemian lifestyle that made him happy. He set a record: 117 nights sleeping outside. In 2003 the number was 115. As Johnny talked, in the distance we could hear the sound of fiddles and banjos. The earth was settling down. A wood duck went winging upriver.

"Already this year," he said, sweeping his hands through the lazy current, "I've slept almost 120 nights outside. I've beat last year's figure and this is only May." (By the end of 2004, we would learn, Johnny's total was 140 nights. If three hurricanes hadn't crossed his area of Florida that fall, the figure would have been 180, he said.)

"When I was a boy," Johnny told us, "I thought the hum of crickets was the sound of stars twinkling. There is an indescribable comfort to lying on the earth, gazing into the sky." Outside, he said, he often hears the first mockingbird or cardinal or dove of the day, calling in the predawn hours.

Americans being treated for depression more than doubled in the decade between 1987 and 1997. The total number of people receiving treatment in the form of prescription drugs like Prozac, Zoloft, and Paxil rose from 1.7 million to 6.3 million. Psychotropic medications, those that affect the mind, are among the most widely prescribed.

According to the National Institute of Mental Health, depression is caused by serious loss, by difficult relationships, by financial problems, by overwhelming stress, by low self-esteem, by pessimism, or by physical changes in the body. Often it runs in families.

*Separated and divorced people show the highest rates of depression;
those who are presently married carry the lowest rates. Major depression
is twice as common among people living alone as among others living
together, in families and communities.*

Now our lives had intersected again with Johnny Dame's,
this time in a supermarket in a strange town. "So what are
you doing here?" he asks us.

"Exploring Pinhook Swamp," I say.

"A great place."

We were standing among perfect, placeless apples
shipped from some apple warehouse to some distribution
center: anonymous apples without history, without origin,
without story. (And without much taste.)

But we are humans of place—of history, origin, story.

We could have been standing by the banks of Falling
Creek, eating dewberries. "We have come from Pinhook,"
we might be telling Johnny, our brother from the South.
We would describe the land to him: *barb cusp briar thistle thorn
antler nib tusk fang tooth spur bristle prick.*

"The land that joins us," we would say. We from above
that wet country, he from below it. "Deer are plentiful
there."

Johnny Dame would invite us to his camp, and we
would go, and when we departed he would hand us a piece
of bark on which he had drawn a map, showing us how to
reach the Suwannee, which we could trace backward, to our
home, so as to skirt Pinhook. The map would be drawn
with two or three shades of clay, and we would marvel at its
artistry.

Autumn

FROM THE JACKSONVILLE airport, alone, I drive to Callahan, then a maze of rural roads westward, 108 to 121 to 94 to 127 to 125. At the concrete bridge across the Saint Marys River I cross into Georgia, my home state. I want to look at the river up close, so at the far side of the bridge I turn left and snake down a rough little road to a landing.

The river is stunning, a midnight blue marbled with amber tannins. It reminds me of a tortoiseshell comb running through white-sand hair. Its sand banks are strong with roots, and from them grow live oak, cypress, palmetto, willow, red maple, sweet gum. How could anybody look once at the Saint Marys River and not fall in love with it? It flows straight into a yearning hole in my heart.

I have flown today from Memphis, Tennessee, back to Pinhook. For ten months we're living in Oxford, Mississippi. I was invited there as writer-in-residence at the university for the academic year. The south Georgia farm is closed for our stint away, and getting to Pinhook is not as easy as a three-hour drive south. I have other business in south Georgia, a book festival and a check on the farm, and I've added a day for the swamp.

A hurricane has been building in the Atlantic, and

although television meteorologists in the airport were saying it will hit farther north, toward Virginia, I am seeing signs of it, that funny roiling of clouds that comes with hurricanes, the sky strewn with cirrus like torn tissue, and the wind picking up. A water strider falls from a titi and glides back toward the bank, tiny skier.

I rinse my face and hands and walk along the sparkleberry banks. Empty plastic bait containers, their lids punctured, are plentiful. I hear a vehicle coming up the access road, and I head to my truck and get it running, ever mindful of being a woman and alone on back roads. Another truck snakes out of the woods road, three men inside. Hunting season isn't here; maybe they're taking a lunchtime ride, scouting. No need to stop and talk.

In a few miles I reach Saint George, Georgia, where the post office has 340 boxes and a bell to ring for service at the counter, and carved above the door to the elementary school is the creed CHOOSE AND RETAIN NOBLE IDEALS. I follow directions to Shack by the Track, a board-and-batten unpainted Cracker-cabin-turned-barbecue-joint. It has picnic tables under trees in the yard. The neon OPEN sign is lit.

A slight woman whose life has worn her down to a gnarled stick is watching television because there's nothing else to do. She gets up and takes my milk shake order at a little sliding window on the porch. She closes the window, but when she finishes the milk shake, she comes out to talk.

"I hope you like it."

"It's delicious. Are these fresh strawberries?"

"Out of a can."

"Are you from Saint George?"

"No, I wasn't born here. I came here with my husband, but he left."

"Why do you stay?"

"I don't know," she says. "Maybe because it's so close to the Florida line. I was born over in Florida. When you get that old Florida sand in your shoes, it's hard to get it out."

Her name is Patsy, but people call her Granny, short for Granny Clampitt on the *Beverly Hillbillies*. That started when she worked at the meatpacking plant, because she used to wear her long hair up in a bun.

"Come back," she says. "The barbecue's real good. People come from all over the place—Fernandina, Jacksonville Beach, Savannah."

"I will," I say. "I didn't know y'all were here."

Thirteen miles on to Moniac, thirty-something to Fargo, the other side of Okefenokee Swamp. The milk shake's so thick I get winded trying to suck it up the straw, which is bigger than any I've ever seen, made for half-gallon-sized drinks, Patsy had told me. Pieces of strawberry get lodged in the straw. The joy of sucking is compromised when you pull air hard and get nothing. I finally resort to using the straw like a spoon.

Many miles later I'm in Taylor, Florida, on the east side of Pinhook Swamp, and I realize I've come the wrong way. I want to hike in at the main Pinhook entrance, off the Blue Ridge, where the Georgia Southern & Florida Railroad runs next to Highway 2, which means I should not have come this far south. My options are to turn around and head back to the no-place called Baxter, which is mostly a check station for truckers avoiding US 1 (trying to get over-loads between Florida and Georgia), or I can head north on Eddy Grade, the dirt-road shortcut to Highway 2. That will be quicker.

I don't stop at the store in Taylor, just drive on north. I

know I'll be hungry later—there's no other place to buy food for God knows how many miles—but I'm ready to get into Pinhook. I want to get prepared for a night there. Even if I sleep supperless.

In half a mile I pull over to let a school bus pass. The bus is barreling along Eddy Grade, fishtailing down the road. That's because the road has turned to a thick rope of deep, sugary sand. It is not the rain-packed road streaming with water that I remember from last spring. I wave at the schoolchildren as they rocket by. I ease on, passing a couple of houses, then reach what appears to be the last house before I enter government pine-timber land. Around the vinyl-sided modular is a yard, if you could call the area a yard, as it hasn't been mowed and maybe never will be, of engineless vehicles and other piles of junk. A chicken is loose in the road, running maniacally along the ditch.

Within three minutes I know I'm in trouble. The shifting, seemingly bottomless road is treacherous; I might as well be driving a tin can as that shiny little two-wheel-drive rental pickup. Momentum gets me through a quarter-mile stretch of concentrated sand, although the truck slows menacingly. Furrows of sand throw the truck sideways and catch at the tires. I keep the gasoline pedal down and grind through the drifts. I feel like a woman I saw once in a driving competition on television, navigating a tricky sand dune. In this case there's no crew running out to physically pull me through the sand traps. For a piece the road hardens again, and then I hit a worse stretch. I'll never make the ten or twelve miles to the highway.

I reach a two-path road turning left and I pull down it and turn around. The path is hard here, wetter. With a running start, I reenter the profoundly sandy Eddy Grade, but without speed, I don't get far. The truck slows, foundering in the sand ridges. I keep the pedal depressed, urging the truck forward. It strains. I press harder, talking now. "Come on, you can do this. Come on, pull harder." But the truck, lacking horsepower and traction, grates to a halt. I shift into low and jam the gas again, crawling forward a few inches. I whip into reverse to try for a running start, but that action only serves for the tires to dig holes for themselves, trapping the truck.

I'd risen at 5 A.M. in Oxford, Mississippi, and driven the wrong way to the Memphis airport. I had reached Pontotoc, a thirty-minute drive in the opposite direction. I whipped a U-turn. Probably I should have accepted the fact that I'd missed my plane, and driven leisurely and safely to Memphis, to wait until the next jet left for Jacksonville. No, I thought I could race time. I drove seventy, eighty, eighty-five. I passed cars like I'd never passed before, as if I trusted speed. All the law officers that morning, luckily, were patrolling elsewhere.

Into Memphis, working my way toward the airport, each red light that caught me added a few more pounds of pressure to my stress level. The plane left in one hour. By now I was hyperventilating. I took a back road I'd never taken to the airport, and it worked; with no time to circle around a parking garage, I parked about a quarter mile away in a parking lot, locked the truck, and grabbed the bags. I was surrounded by a maze of buildings, highways, and parking lots. "Excuse me, which way is the terminal?" I breathlessly asked a woman in the lot, who pointed. I started running across a road, then a grassy area, then another road, then a parking garage, then the eight-lane road in front of the terminal where the big shuttle buses ferry passengers interminably to and fro.

When I got to the gate with no minutes to spare, the airline clerk was closing the jetport. But she had seen me running down the concourse and hustled me on the plane, where, being the last passenger on, I could choose any open seat in the house. Six hours after I left our Oxford home without breakfast, I arrived in Jacksonville, rented a sissy truck, loaded my luggage, ate a platter of fried grouper at the first restaurant I found, and headed west.

The events of the day cling to me as I get out and consider my predicament. I am impossibly stuck. Using my hands I scoop sand from in front of the tires, trying to clear enough passage that the truck can purchase solid road bottom and move forward. I get back in, try driving gear, then low, and when I move a few inches (although I cannot tell if I am moving forward or downward), I get back out and again rake sand from in front of the tires. I try again, and this time the truck moves not at all, through I rev the engine urgently.

I get out again and shut the door. Eddy Grade stretches for miles northward, in a straight line, and extends at least a mile behind me. No house is in sight. Who knows when another vehicle will happen along? Maybe everybody local knows not to travel this road without four-wheel drive. Then I relax. On this particular day being stuck is likely the best thing that can happen. I beat the odds all morning, and if I keep pressing my luck, I might finally hurt myself. Heck, I can hike off the road right where I am, into thick woods that rise on all sides, and spend the night. I have everything I need.

I drink a bottle of water dry. I change into a pair of shorts in the middle of the road and put on hiking boots. I stick a writing pad and pen in my back pocket and stride south.

Less than five minutes later, for no reason at all, I twist around, and far in the distance, a truck barrels toward me. Unbelievable. I turn back. When the truck reaches me, two men stop and get out of an old Chevy eight-cylinder. They are roofers from Callahan, come to scout out trees for deer stands, since bow-hunting season starts in three days. Their vehicle is two-wheel drive too, they say, and they've come all the way through Eddy Grade by the grace of speed, truck weight, and a set of wide, heavy tires.

The bow hunters give me a ride back to the last house and enlist the help of David Bryant, whom we meet there, a man whose hair, though paling, shines coppery red beneath a Ford cap. He agrees without hesitation to pull my truck out with his pickup, a small four-by-four Toyota that, like its owner, has seen a lot of wear.

"When you live out here," he says, "you learn to carry everything in your truck you might need. I got rope, chain." He has a wire cage back there too, and a lot of empty beer cans. This isn't his house. He has come to bring two roosters to his friend. He is a hunter and a woods rambler; used to hunt bear when it was legal, and has seen plenty in Pinhook.

"Let's go get her," David says, and invites me to sit up front with him, crammed beside a cooler in the floor of the passenger's side. The two roofers pile onto the back, along with two young boys, one of whom is David's grandson. "I just saw you on the road," the boy says. "I was on the school bus." The other boy is Bo, who is maybe fifteen, and they tell me he will walk through the woods barefoot, right across palmetto roots and cypress knees, and will pick up moccasins in his hand.

Characteristics that link humans:
- *The similarity of our physiology*
- *Breath*
- *The need for water*
- *The vulnerability of the life within us*
- *The drive to defend ourselves*
- *The move toward satiation from thirst, hunger, and discomfort*
- *The need for touch*
- *The capabilities of our minds*
- *Many, many senses*
- *Curiosity*
- *Imagination—an urge and ability to create*
- *The capacity to communicate*
- *Mutual attraction and desire*
- *The power of our love to overwhelm hate and fear*
- *Our ability to fully feel this love*
- *A quest for intimacy*
- *Spirit*

To remember these is to remind ourselves of the futility of human isolation. Know too that black bears apparently do not have to remind themselves of their mutuality and common goodness.

"What can you tell me about Pinhook Swamp?" I ask David.

"Back years ago we made moonshine in there," he says. And stops.

"You've tasted moonshine made in Pinhook Swamp?" I'm thinking of the gallberry honey.

He stares at me, incredulous. He has sky-blue eyes and a pale red wraparound cowboy mustache. "Tasted?" he says. "I've made it."

The men on the back have somehow heard the conversation through the open window. One of them sticks his head forward. "Watch out, now," he says. "Don't tell her where the still is!" The men on the back of the truck laugh into the wind.

"I can right now go get you all the moonshine you want," says David.

"I wish I wanted some." I will later learn that East Coast Lumber Company, which built many trams into the timberlands of Okefenokee and Pinhook, officially called their rail line the Watertown Northern Rail Road Moonshine Line.

"They've cut roads in the swamp now. And ditches. They tried to drain the water out. But in them little creeks in there, that's where all the fish grow. Fish in little creeks used to be plentiful—you could get a mess of bream in no time—but there ain't that many anymore. I think it's because of them ditches."

We are almost upon my little gold truck, embedded in the road. David's pickup begins to grumble in the sand, and I ask him if the tow will be a problem.

"Me have a problem?" he says. "I'm still in two-wheel." He positions his truck and ties a canvas towline between the chassis, and in no time my truck is up on the grassy, hard two-path road. Instead of pulling me back all the way to his friend's house, he'll lead me out through the woods. We stand a few more minutes around the trucks.

"I was raised out here in these woods," David says, more

expansive now and perhaps enchanted with the way I hang on to his words, writing them down. "I've seen a bunch of stuff. I've seen bear tracks this big." His thumbs and fore-fingers describe a circle the size of a dinner plate.

"How big a bear makes a track like that?" I ask.

"Eight, nine hundred pound," he says. "When I first saw this bear, a long time ago, he stood about this high." He held his hand up toward his chest. "He could scratch to the top of the truck to mark his territory. Now if I got up on tiptoe and held my hand up, I probably couldn't reach his mark."

"Unh."

"Have you ever seen a bear catch a hog?" he asks. Nobody here has. "Bear likes pork. A hog don't have a chance around a bear." He pauses for effect and asks one of the roofers to throw him a beer from the cooler. "Y'all are welcome to a beer," he says. "They cold and all. If you care for one."

The rest of us watch him pop a can open.

"We was out here hog hunting," he says. "I was probably seventeen or eighteen years old. Daddy went to Lake City and got hunt permits late in the afternoon, and we went in. We hadn't turned no dogs loose yet. We were pretty deep in the swamp when we heard a hog a-squealing, not too far away. We got to where it was and saw a bear had a hog. It was a seventy- to eighty-pound shoat. That bear weighed about four hundred pound." He pauses, takes a draw. "That's a sight not a lot of people seen."

"I'd like to see it."

"I'm sixty year old," he explained. "I ride through the woods a lot. I keep up yards for people, and when I get done I get me a cold beer and ride through the woods. I see a lot. If you want me to, I'll take my grandson home and I'll ride you through the woods and tell you all the stories you want to hear about Pinhook Swamp."

"I better get on," I say, "and figure out a place to camp. Thank you."

The roofers have missed their chance to scout, but they don't seem to mind. They'll come back after work tomorrow, they say.

Nest eggs are set aside, placed back under laying hens to be sat upon, to produce more chicks. Money set aside for retirement is part of a nest egg.

This idea of setting aside for the future—for hard times, for continuation of the species, for gift, for charity, for old age, for children, for others, for later enjoyment—is ancient. It's not only a human idea. Squirrels set aside for winter, caching. Panthers and alligators stash uneaten portions of large prey and return to it. Understanding the tenuousness of life on this planet, or any planet, why would it not be a prudent thing, a trait evolved for preservation of self and species, to set aside entire landscapes of wild land? Not to hoard, but for our survival.

It's late and I don't head up to the north side of Pinhook. The fire tower where Raven and I camped in the spring is spooky in its emptiness, so I drive farther south, to a primitive campground outside Gum Swamp Wilderness, in Osceola National Forest. The campground is full of tents and campers, but empty of people, except for a man who blares up on a four-wheeler to check me out.

"We've had some theft," he explains. He tells me the camps have been set up in anticipation of bow season; the hunters are saving places and will arrive after work on Friday.

"We've been coming here twenty-seven years," he says,

"for the start of the season. One man's been coming fifty years. He hasn't come yet this year. I don't know if something's wrong—sick maybe, or if he's died.

"By the way, this camping spot you're at gets wet if it rains." I'm parked next to a water lily pond lined with scraggly, unrestrained shrubs. Behind the pond the woods start. "For some reason, water flows from ever' which way right down here."

"Have you heard the forecast?"

"I haven't heard it's gon' rain. You'll be okay if it don't rain. My wife is here with me. Come up if you need anything."

What I need is a tent. For weight's sake on the airplane I opted not to bring it, thinking the weather cool enough for sleeping alfresco. Already I'm slapping mosquitoes.

When darkness falls I lay my pad and bag on the bare ground. Mosquitoes quickly find me. I get up and zip my bug shirt over my face, but the night is hot, too hot to be wearing a shirt and veil inside a down-filled bag that's warm even in zero-degree weather. I worry about snakes too. Think how many months they follow their own routes and trails, unseen on the ground, in pilgrimages from the uplands to the water. I may be lying smack in the rattlesnake road. Or the moccasin path. It's a thrill-less thought, and after a while I get up and walk gingerly, barefoot, across the dark, torn ground to the truck and sleep restlessly, wadded in the cab.

Voice from the Wilderness

THE WATER IS good. Drink of it.
The wind is pure and good. Breathe full of it.
Behold, all creatures are accounted for. That you
  know them.
The plants have returned to their places. Yea.
In your towns the people are accounted for.
Behold. It has come to this.
In your towns the people are gathered together in
  lives of marvel.
Yea, it has come to this.

Taylor, Florida

THE NEXT MORNING I aim for Taylor Store, to catch the unemployed gentlemen who surely sit around together of a morning, talking up the day. First the water lilies blooming on the pond deter me, and then when I get out to the flatwoods, I sit in the blind the truck makes and watch birds in the fire-cleaned forest, mainly a family of red-bellied woodpeckers. The world is lovely. Of course I would have fallen in love so very long ago with it—with its flatwoods and swamps, its sloughs and sandhills. Of course I would have lived in service to it.

At the store a red-and-blue neon sign says OPEN, alongside a poster for ice—$1.09 PLUS TAX. WE HAVE BAIT SHRIMP NOW. Two small goats graze in the side yard.

The owner of the store is there, as is her husband. I wash out my traveling cup and get a cup of coffee, not that I'm a coffee drinker, clink two quarters into the coffee till, and buy a bottle of milk and a honey bun. I tell the woman, who has curled strawberry-blond hair, what I am in Taylor for, and ask her where the coffee drinkers are.

"Nobody has showed up yet today," Trudy says. "Maybe they're working. But I doubt it." She grins at me.

"I'm gonna sit outside on the bench and see if anybody comes along I can talk to," I say.

"You shouldn't wait long."

The store is situated at the intersection of the road to Glen Saint Mary, Florida, and the road through the national forest toward Georgia, which turns to sand (bad sand, remember) just north. Most everybody has to slow up when they pass the store. "There comes one now," she says, gazing out the window, which has black iron bars across it. A farm truck pulls up and a man gets out, walks to a white truck parked at the gas tank, and opens its door.

"What is Homer doing in my truck?" the woman asks me.

I go outside, sit on the church pew slid up against the store, and pour as much milk into my tall cup as there is coffee. The storekeeper's husband comes out and eases down at the picnic table on the other side of the door. He remembers me from last spring when we stopped and took a picture of the store. His name is Green. The other man, the one named Homer, sits down with him at the picnic bench. Homer is wearing faded jeans and a collared shirt that is not tucked in. He has a camouflage baseball cap on his head, and a pair of Red Wing boots on his feet. One of his pant legs is caught on top of his boot.

"I finally got my turnips planted," Homer says to Green.

"I thought you planted them turnips last week," Green replies.

"I never got to it." Silence from Green, morning all around. "They better make good, much as I paid for them."

"How much?" Green asks.

"Five fifty a pound."

Green stares. "That's expensive turnips."

The morning is unimaginably beautiful—a tinge of cool-ness, a shade of blue to the far distance, an autumn sun-shine so liquid you want to drink it. Like thin, bright honey.

Trudy comes out. "You better stay out of my truck," she says, squeezing Homer's shoulders. She has an infectious giggle. "Homer, ain't you got stories about Pinhook? She's writing a piece." She glances toward me, where I have so far been a fixture of this incredible morning. Trudy doesn't know my name so I am simply a pronoun. My name's too hard to pronounce and remember anyway, so I don't bother to say it.

Homer looks toward me. I smile, pad and pen balanced on one leg. "Are you a hunter?"

"I'm out there." He grins. "I ain't killed nothing yet."

"You take your glasses off, you'd be able to see," Green says.

"I guess so, looking through a scope. I can't remember to take 'em off."

"Daddy takes his off to read!" says Trudy.

A younger man arrives, a strong, deeply tanned man in his thirties. He's wearing a gold chain around his neck and very clean, light-colored shorts and shirt. Nobody intro-duces anybody, but from the greetings I learn his name is Ross. He sits at the picnic table as well.

"Do you all realize what a great place you live in?" I ask them. "With all the pavement and cities and building going on, you live in one of the wildest places left in Florida, maybe the whole South. It's really like a place out of time."

The newcomer, Ross, shushes me good-naturedly. "Sssshhh. Keep that part to yourself."

"Too many people moving here now," Green says.

"That government land won't ever be sold," says Homer.

"I remember when I first moved out here," says Ross, "you could drive that road right there at night and you wouldn't pass a car all the way to Glen Saint Mary. Not a car."

"That's right," agrees Homer. "If you broke down after midnight, you had a long walk home." He remembers another fact. "Forty years ago, we had a hundred and something voters out here in this district. Now we have four hundred."

"My God, you're eighty-two!" Trudy exclaims. Homer whoops, and says to me, aside, "Not really." Everybody is laughing.

"What's the road like now?" I ask Ross.

"Car, car, car," he says. "I don't know where so many cars come from. I've seen 'em three wide out there. 'Bout to run into each other trying to get where they're going. I said to myself, 'Whoa, I'm on the road at the wrong time.'"

"It's people moving in. They're getting an acre or two and moving a trailer in," says Trudy.

"You don't have a post office out here, do you?"

"No, they bring the mail out. Our address is Sanderson."

"We get our mail from Sanderson, our phone from Maclenny, and our electric from Georgia," Homer offers.

"We're a tri-metro area," quips Ross.

Human linkages: neighborhood potlucks, meetings of societies, bingo nights, coffeehouses and bars and restaurants, gallery walks, town meetings, dinner parties, cookouts, concerts, support groups, book clubs, subway and train and bus stations, airports, baseball diamonds, sports bleachers, square dances, art exhibits, parties.

The Taylorans are fascinated with their descriptions of how removed they are, as if reminding themselves. Obvious to me is the fact they love being at the end of a road, backed up to a wild place, next to the Georgia line. I want details, although I am already aware that theirs is another world, not necessarily a pretty one or a monied one. It is one that is very different from most of the world.

"You can't use a cell phone out here," Ross tells me. "You get almost to Glen Saint Mary before it will pick up."

"And we don't have a pay phone," Trudy says. "We used to have one, but somebody one night got the bright idea to rob it and busted it up. It only had three dollars in it." She giggles. "That was three or four years ago. The phone company wants fifteen hundred dollars to bring another one. That's too much." She apparently is not angered by the loss of the pay phone at her store, simply mystified by life's ironies.

"Telemarketers call me about a new package on my cell phone. 'No way,' I tell them. 'I can't even use the damn thing here,'" says Ross.

Not long ago I attended a benefit contra dance for a western Massachusetts grammar school, Greenfield Center. Old-time dancing has been revived among folk-music aficionados; as the term folk implies, this form of dancing cuts through racial, social, and economic divisions. "Contra" is a form of old-time dance executed in long lines of couples. I arrived early for the Sunday afternoon hop, and two middle-school students collected my eight dollars and stamped my hand.

But this was a family dance, I learned. I was accustomed to contra dances where adult men and women promenaded, gazed into each other's eyes as they executed the "gypsy," chained, and cast off to tunes like "Sally

Goodin" and "The Curly Headed Ploughboy." As many children as adults were on the floor, the youngest of them about two years old.

The caller taught a dance that started with everyone making a huge circle about the Grange, and that included the touching of different body parts (elbow, knee, head) to the floor. Wild Asparagus began to play, its piano and fiddle and bodhran raising their lively music into the room. After a few dances, the Grange was overflowing with dancers of all ages, sizes, and colors, whooping and stomping and twirling. The music rose and rose, carrying us in its energy. I danced with grandmothers and with little boys and with fathers bouncing infants on their hips and with toddlers, bending far in order to swing them.

Somewhere in the middle of the evening, I thought, This is what wholeness looks like: a dance hall full of people grinning and stamping and singing and laughing. This is the opposite of fragmentation.

A small pickup pulls up, and a man who tends toward the dapper minces toward us. None of these neighbors appears to have anything better to do this perfectly lovely fall morning than sit at the store and talk. Perhaps because of our little knot of people, more stop, and perhaps because of me they stay longer. They want to know what magazine I'm writing for, what I write about. They're not suspicious; they're jovial and full of imp.

"How you doing, Sheldon?"

"'Bout to outgrow every damn thing I got," Sheldon says. He resembles Elvis. He is wearing a bright red shirt and a pair of new blue jeans, with docksiders. He limps.

"I'm upset over that protest," he says. That gets everybody's attention.

"Protest?"

"About Budweiser burying a pipeline to my place." He

says this without a trace of a smile. "I was looking forward to metered service." He sits down in a chair I haven't noticed.

"You gon' have a heart attack if you keep laughing," Trudy says to Homer.

"And I ain't gonna give you mouth-to-mouth," says Green. He turns to me. "He's already had one heart attack up here. And a stroke."

"At the store?"

"At the store."

"We may not save him next time."

A man and a dog come walking down the road. "Here comes Flash and Ryan," Trudy says.

"I believe Flash is faster than Ryan this morning." I wonder which is which.

"He's got a trot going."

"He better keep that horny thing away from my dogs," says Green. "One of the girls is in heat."

"I've got work to do," Trudy says good-naturedly. "Unlike the rest of you."

"We're making a new civilization," Green says to her. "Where the women work and the men don't." She laughs, gets in the truck to leave, and the radio blares. She turns it down and hollers at Homer. "You better be glad company's here," she says.

Homer chuckles. "I turned the heat up full blast too," he says, low. Trudy drives off.

"She's gonna be pissed," says Green.

The more intimate the human relationship, the more functional. The more linkage it provides. Intimacy, the fuel that nourishes our humanity. We can examine for ourselves which linkages are most functional:

- *Those in which we are able to share our deepest sorrows, joys, and needs*
- *Those in which we are able and courageous enough to tell the truth*
- *Those in which we feel safe, feel at home*
- *Those that encourage us to be ourselves*
- *Those in which we respect and are respected*
- *Those in which we listen and are listened to*
- *Those free of patterns of abuse, neglect, deceit, and addiction*
- *Those in which we may reveal both our flaws and successes, failures and talents*
- *Those that propel us toward the lives we dream for ourselves*

"Yeah, half the East Coast is damn near full," says Ross.

"That's the truth."

"I saw a picture taken at night by a satellite or something, and most of the East Coast was lit up. This was about the only place still dark."

"That was taken by the Huddle telescope," says Sheldon. He meant the Hubble. "If you got your windows on your computer, you can get on it and see right down to your house."

"Walter Gaines, he got right down to the cedar tree in his front yard," says Ross. The men must have the same informant.

"You could zoom in and see the numbers on that mailbox there," says Sheldon. He gets up to go in the store, and Green follows to wait on him.

"What was the most amazing sight you ever saw in Pinhook?" I ask Ross.

"That big ole buck I shot." He chortles with pride.

"How big was it?"

"Eight point."

"What about the one you missed?" Homer asks. He knows a story I don't know.

"Homer," Ross says, "we don't want to talk about the ones we let go."

"I ain't goin' in the swamp no more," says Ryan. He is a tall, gaunt man in his forties who rarely speaks. Flash is the dog. "I done got lost. I ain't goin' in no more." I ask how he got lost, but he only sits there, looking away.

"Reckon how many gallons of moonshine they made out there?" I ask, trying to guide the information. The men sit around shaking their heads. The number is unfathomable.

"Used to, you could sit on the store's porch and see the stills firing up. That was the old store, the one that burnt. It had a porch."

"How?" I ask.

"How what?"

"How could you see a still firing up?"

"It used to be cooked with lighterd," Homer says. "That smoked real bad when you first lit it, like burning tires. After that it was kerosene. When they started using gas that's when moonshine picked up."

"Why?"

"It don't smoke." I nod my head slowly, understanding.

"I remember a still at Shingle Pond," says Ross.

"I got married one night and they put me in jail for making moonshine the next night," Homer says. "I never had to serve time—they let me off on probation." He pauses. "My brother pulled time twice. My uncle went to prison four times for it."

If intimacy is function, then for a wild place intimacy is:
  - *Diversity of species*
  - *Ability of land to feed, water, and shelter its creatures*
  - *Uncompromised natural processes of production and purification*
  - *Promise of continuation of species*

Then there's intimacy with a wild place. By choice we can ignore or honor this connection. I believe that intimacy with place is an important part of being human, that in fact it helps define our humanness. Part of being fully human requires engagement with our places. Which brings us back toward wholeness.

Sheldon comes back out of Taylor Store with a six-pack of Budweiser. It is not even ten in the morning.

"I got the one with the expiration date going out at midnight tonight," he jokes. "So I'll have to drink it all today." He makes a beeline to his pickup and leaves.

"Not much moonshine making anymore," Homer says.

"A little wine making."

"Puddy Crews makes the best wine I ever had. He even makes persimmon wine. But the best is grape."

"And it's legal."

"I've seen wine made in jail," says Ryan.

"Hell, that's not wine," says Homer. "That's buck."

A family van slowly pulls into the lot, up to the front of the store, and I see three women in it.

"Y'all do have women out here," I say. "I was beginning to think Pinhook Swamp was all men. Except for Trudy."

Trudy has come back from her errand. "Not these," she says. "These are foreigners."

Two well-dressed women get out. I see one of them place a Bible on the dashboard as she alights.

"Is that a deer?" the one driving says to the other. We can hear them.

"No, that's a goat," the woman laughs. They approach the storefront in their heels, chuckling.

"The goats eat all the trash around here," somebody says to them.

"She thought it was a deer," the woman says.

"I didn't know. It's little for a goat."

"Hunting'd be a lot easier if it was," Homer says. The women pause a minute, then push open the door. Trudy gets up to wait on them, and while they are inside I ask the men what reason would bring three well-dressed women to Taylor. None of them knows. In a few minutes the women emerge with sodas. I ask where they are from.

"Two from Jacksonville, one from Maclenny."

"What brings you to Taylor?"

"I used to be from Taylor," the one with hair dyed coal black says. "I'm Curtis Lawrence's sister." The men nod. They know him and seem to remember her.

"So you're back visiting."

"We're Jehovah's Witnesses."

"You're visiting, then, I guess." She agrees, and the women pass toward their car. The men stay perfectly still and silent, reserving comment. When the missionaries have crept out of the uneven parking area, back onto hardtop, one of the men says, "I recognize the black-headed one. She works at the liquor store in town at night."

"That's where it is! I knew I knew her from somewhere."

"The liquor store? Do Jehovah's drink?"

"I didn't think so."

"Well, I gotta go," Homer says. "I'm taking my lawn mower to Lake City. It's not mowing level." He moves toward his old truck.

"You sure you're level when you're mowing?"

Homer laughs. "Well, I *was* thinking about getting me a cup holder welded on it."

"You ought to see how he drinks," someone says to me, after Homer carefully pulls out of the lot and whines down the road.

"How's that?"

"He don't take sips. It's like drinking tea."

Anyone stalled all day in front of Taylor Store, speaking to the patrons as they arrived and departed, would soon know what fabric this community was made of, woven together as it was by distance, by heat, by alcohol, by hunting, by poverty, by vast swamp. At Taylor Store you find out all you need to know about human nature and life. Sit there long enough and you become Taylor, Florida. Sit there long enough and you might sew a life together that begins to make sense.

NOAH'S ISLAND

NOT A TRAIL. Old tram running out to somewhere nobody goes. A country characterized by shrubs. Walled by dog hobble, gallberry, sweet bay magnolia, wax myrtle. Thick and impassable. Until the shrubs converge. Catbrier sewing it all together with its thorn needles.

Six miles back to the highway. Fifteen miles to a store. Forty miles to a hospital. A thousand to my husband. This tram unmarked.

Early fall and everything full of berries. Candyweed on the moist ground. Tiny, soft woodland grass, one and a half inches high. Sundews like big chiggers, like red coins all over the ground. Their miniature traps sweetly cocked. Lavender flowers of smooth meadow beauty. So fragile the petals fall if you brush them.

Pileated woodpecker far off, calling. *Ha, ha, ha, ha, ha.* Lands in a snag. Landscape of snags, standing dead, burned by some recent fire. Snag land. Landscape of shrubs. Eye-level landscape. On tiptoe I see above it. Forever.

Time of spiders. Hundreds, strung between shrubs. Head level. Old tattered webs, new webs, gilt webs. Which means no one my height has passed here in whenever.

Passage of animals. Stretches of mud, canvas of tracks.

The black bear was walking on all fours. Place where an alligator dragged its tail. Slithering through a knee-high arch into the tram ditch alongside. Sharp three-pronged alligator tracks. Bobcat. Raccoon. Deer or hog, I can't tell the difference in sphagnum.

Noise in dry leaves. I stop. Cottonmouth moccasin approaches. I slam my feet down so the earth trembles. Moccasin trembles. The boy Bo would pick it up, but not me. Snake flings six inches of upper body into the air. To look bigger. Looks big enough already.

Gallberry switch in front of my face to catch the webs. Stick in my hand, weaving through the grass in front of me. Announcing passage to snakes. Me walking with binoculars, backpack, pad and pencil. The gun in its holster against my ribs. Marking me. Embarrassing me. An imprinted fear. Two sticks. Spiders scurry up threads, seeing me coming. They are not without safety measures.

In and in and in. Sun lowering in western sky. Faster. To get to wherever I'm going. To where this land opens out. Noah's Island. A couple of red-bellied woodpeckers.

More tracks. Bear scat. Not such a big pile. Not so fresh. Wet feet in a couple of places where the water converges.

Over an hour walking. Slow. Hard. One mile, two miles.

Finally a body of water. Like a pond. More trees. Crescent of pines in the distance. More water. What they mean by *island* is trees. So I find it. And the walking is easier again. Road veers right. Another kind of grass I do not know. More walking.

Suddenly a new sound. Not birds. A *wonk, wonk, wonk* I recognize. Baby alligators.

The danger of mother alligators. Good Lord, they'll kill you if they think you're after their babies. Take the gun out.

Hold it ready. Creep to the edge of the water. Still two slash pines between the water and me. I don't want to kill anything. Just see them. I'd run all day before I'd shoot.

Baby alligators like little spotted spoons. Stirring the water. *Wonking* in sheer terror. Hiding in flotsam and jetsam. Eight or nine of them. Maybe more. This is Noah's Island. Place where alligators hatch and begin. But there's more than two of everything, Noah.

Center of Pinhook. Everything Pinhook is, is here.

Another sign to turn is the big orange sun. Bottom of it level with the horizon.

Back the same way. Dusk now. Racing night. Time the crepuscular animals emerge. Will bears follow you? Alligators drag you under. The length of the tusks of wild boars. Apex of sun's disk finally gone. Back and back and back.

Candyweed, meadow beauty, gallberry, titi, dog hobble. Sweet bay magnolia. Slash pine, pond pine. The same scurrying, scrambling spiders. Tracks and slides and scat. No snake where I saw it. The world turning to night. Down and down. Me running.

When I reach the road darkness falls.

I can breathe.

PERPETUITY

And God said, "This is the token of the covenant
which I make between me and you and every
living creature that is with you, for perpetual
generations: . . . the waters shall no more
become a flood to destroy all flesh."
—GENESIS 9:12–15

FROM THE CHRISTIAN religion of my childhood, I learned
a great understanding of forever. Forever came after we
died and meant that nothing ever ended. Life was finite;
forever was infinite. Forever was longer than all the grains
of sand on all the beaches of the earth. Forever meant
longer than any one of us could imagine.

The preservation of Okefenokee, Pinhook, and Osceola
forever is a pact of faith. The oldest human document, the
Hindu Veda, is a pact of faith with its people that continues
to this day. In the United States, though the Constitution is
amended, it still clings to tenets laid out in 1787, following
the intent of the law. A pact with our people.

Forever means that longer than I can imagine, without
end, beyond any death, the landscape will remain.

Most any intent, however, can be changed by a world gone awry. Always a tenet can be broken—a father leaves his children, a wife leaves her husband. A woman specifies in her last will and testament that, above all, she wants a grove of trees she owns to be saved. She thinks she has done what needs to happen. A will is contested, and what the judge rules is not what the deceased wanted. The grove is cut. A farm a man loved all his life is sold by his children. A piece of our Osceola National Forest was stolen back by some department of transportation for a rest area.

We say we are great believers in private-property rights in this country, but at any time a person's property could get taken for a road, a bridge, a building, a runway—if the project is deemed to be for the common good.

I have another example of a broken covenant. The U.S. government is breaking a tenet with its people nationally by logging in our national forests. These are forests that all of us own, and the logging continues, at a loss both financial and ecological.

Let me explain. In 1996, $800 million was appropriated from the General Fund of the U.S. Treasury for the timber-sale program. The Forest Service spent another $532 million. Logging generated $535 million in receipts, none of which returned to the General Fund. You can figure the loss yourself. We, the taxpayers, are paying for the administration of timber sales, for logging-road construction and repair, and for the damage occasioned by mudslides, floods, and fires directly or indirectly caused by logging in *our* national forests.

Our modern definition of *perpetuity* scares me. When we save a place *for perpetuity*, do we really mean for a time greater than all the grains of sand on all the beaches of the world? When are we going to recognize that carbon dioxide filtration and water purification and food production for wildlife and humans will always be the highest and best common good? When are we going to understand with our minds and with our laws that the widening highway will lead to our demise, but natural places will always sustain us?

When we proclaim that a wild land has been saved, do we mean the foreseeable future? Do we mean only until today's ideals pass out of history's understanding? Or do we really mean forever?

Now the deed to Pinhook Swamp is held by the people of the United States. Congratulations.

Is there a benevolence in you, as citizen, as patriot, to love your land and let it be, or is your name on this deed no better than the forest investment timber company developer corporate property rights capitalist who sees land as dollar figures? And who is disappointed that there was not more to take? That the land was inhospitable to humans? That it couldn't be turned to quick growth, because he and she always wanted something growing, preferably a bank account and/or a stock market portfolio? Who always wanted something producing?

Can you see the riches in fetterbush and bay?

Psalm for Pinhook

LET US PUT our minds together and give thanks
for the wild abandon of woods,
for a shrubby bog,
a great swamp and pine country
joined as one.
As they were in the beginning.
By no act of our hands shall we transgress against it,
lest we lose sight of ourselves,
creatures of Earth.
Let us consider each species of its kind valuable:
the whole an idea,
but the individual a present moment unfolding.
For the sake of our souls, and for the desire
yearning from every bud tip and teat,
from invisible cells and hives of larvae,
shuffling inside the fragile cups of eggs
and the warm bellies of mothers.
Let us act according to a tree's wishes
and not our own.
Let us help when we can,
and be gone when we are a hindrance
to the civilization of biota.

Let us praise the living. And then the dead,
who nourish the living.
Let us not forsake possibility.
Let us befriend and tame fear
until we are clothed in the unrent garments
of honor
and repay with our toil
all that we needlessly took.

A Vision

SO FAR 120,000 of 170,600 acres have been purchased in the Pinhook Corridor. We must keep adding to this state of wild. There is more to go. Let's purchase what's left of Pinhook Swamp. Let's add Impassable Bay and Sandlin Bay to the Pinhook Corridor. To displace people from their land is unethical, although the military and the federal transportation system and big corporations have done it forever, just as we displaced the Native Americans, so let's get this timber acreage before it gets broken up and sold off.

Let's get really visionary and make a place big enough to bring the large carnivores back. Let us make a sanctuary. Let's welcome the big cats and the red wolves home.

There is more to go.

Although DuPont had publicly abandoned its mine proposal in 1999, for years the ninety million dollars called for in the no-mining agreement had not been found and fear of mining had not lessened. Then on August 27, 2003, DuPont Corporation donated the proposed titanium mine site on the edge of Okefenokee Swamp—nearly sixteen thousand acres of land—to the Conservation Fund, one of the largest land-conservation donations ever. The organization added five thousand acres to the refuge and kept eleven thousand under its protection. People all over the world celebrated. One more piece of the puzzle was in place.

Now more of Trail Ridge must be protected and added to Okefenokee Swamp.

Let's end the logging in Dixon Memorial State Forest and begin to return it to its original wildness. Let's replant the golf course in trees.

Then let's purchase the cutover uplands surrounding the swamp, so that we may restore the longleaf pine ecosystem there, ensuring native homes for the creatures endemic to longleaf pine and threatened by its agonizing demise, the gopher tortoises and indigo snakes and red-cockaded woodpeckers and Bachman's sparrows.

Let's retain habitat for creatures who migrate between the two ecosystems. Some live in the swamp but require uplands for reproduction—turtles, for egg laying, for example. Some live in the uplands but require wetlands for reproduction—like flatwoods salamanders.

Here's the vision: Let's preserve a landscape that encompasses both uplands and lowlands, a place as vast as the New Jersey Pine Barrens, at its center the Pinhook pocosin. Let's join the Pinhook Corridor to the Appalachian Trail, then take it on to New Brunswick, crossing the continent with the "Atlantic MegaLinkage" that Dave Foreman, director of the Rewilding Institute, proposes. Let's preserve a landscape large enough to preserve our hopes and dreams of wildness, wild enough to contain a natural history that defines who we are. Let's fill it as Noah filled the Ark, with the creatures of the southeastern coastal plains, limpkins and bald eagles and Florida panthers and southeastern shrews and pinewoods tree frogs and big brown bats. Let's reconnect, restore, rewild.

Dear friend, no act would be wiser than to save a large wild land so that evolution may continue, uninterrupted by our fiddling with it. Dear neighbor to Pinhook, how blessed you are and how lucky to be able to live with such wildness at your door. Dear Senator, believe me when I say that no legacy we can leave in this postindustrial age will be greater, more noble, than that of a wild land left to restore itself. Dear President of the United States, this will be an accomplishment greater than any, a landmark.

We don't need more human names and edifices attached to this state of wildness—oh, keep the human record unrecorded there.

And when the last tract of land is added that makes the Pinhook puzzle a beautiful platter again, it will become a land bridge in a sea of civilization. Over which our progeny may someday cross.

For the sake of humanity, widen and strengthen the bridge.

ACKNOWLEDGMENTS

SOME OF THE names used in this book are fictitious. All of the people are real.

Much gratitude goes to:

Carolyn Servid and Dorik Mechau of the Island Institute for offering me a writing residency in Sitka, Alaska, for the month of April 2003, where I began this little book. The librarians of Kettleson Public Library and Sheldon-Jackson College Library in Sitka. The good, open-armed people of Sitka for their kindness to us.

The University of Mississippi and John and Renée Grisham for the writer residency (2003–2004) that allowed me time and space to devote myself to writing, where I finished this project. The fabulous town of Oxford, Mississippi—all the genius and friendship and imagination and help its people offered.

Larry Thompson for dedication to the Pinhook Osceola and Greater Okefenokee project, and for all the ways he participated in the making of this book. William Metz for being a top-notch guide and proponent of the wildland corridor.

Christa Frangiamore for a conversation that led to the subject of Pinhook.

Raven Burchard, Chip Campbell, Judy Hancock, Larry D. Harris, Milton Hopkins, Kyle Jones, Phil Nieswander, Cindy Thompson, Chris Trowell, Frankie Snow, and Breeze VerDant for research on Pinhook and other information vital to this book.

The people of the environs of Taylor, Florida, for all the stories they told me.

The United States Forest Service for buying Pinhook Swamp and giving it back to all of us. All other government agencies who are assisting.

Activists, biologists, and citizens who have worked to make sure the O2O happens, including and not limited to: Edwin Abbey, Gene Bernofsky, Rex Boner, Phyllis Bowen, Linda Bremer, Carol Browner, Chip Campbell, Joy Campbell, Don Cohrs, Sam Collier, Maurice Coman, Jim Cox, Jeremy Dixon, Gary Drury, George Foley, Manley Fuller, Judy Hancock, Larry D. Harris, Richard Hilsenbeck, Marian Hilliard, Karen Howard, Kyle Jones, Randy Kautz, Jo Knight, Steve Knight, Jim Lyle, Josh Marks, Bill McQuilkin, William Metz, Phil Nieswander, Reed Noss, Don Perkuchin, Andrew Schock, Becky Shortland, Bob Simons, Larry Thompson, Chris Trowell, Genna and Roger Wangsness, David White, Stephen Williams, Sheila Willis, George Willson, and John Winn. Members and funders of the POGO Coalition.

To Suzan Satterfield and Turner South, for their beautiful production of *The Pinhook Swamp Puzzle*, which aired on the show *The Natural South*. Also Becky Buzogany, Allen Facemire, and Walter James.

Catherine Paige West, who let me read her master's thesis, which she completed while at the University of Georgia, on Pinhook: "Wilderness Defined by Human

Action: Understanding the Relationship Between Culture, Praxis and Nature."

John Harris of the Monandnock Institute in New Hampshire, and his wife, Susie, who gave my family a place to stay during the crucial days of revising the manuscript.

Margo Baldwin, Collette Leonard, Erin Hanrahan, and the other good people of Chelsea Green Publishing, who want a wilder future for America.

The able editing of Robin Dutcher, Robin Catalano, and Laura Jorstad. Thank you.

Molly O'Halloran, an excellent cartographer.

Dave Borland, poet, ecologist, and good friend, for keen thinking about these pages.

The people of the Wildlands Project (reconnect, restore, rewild), who are "designing and helping create systems of interconnected wilderness areas that can sustain the diversity of life." John Davis, Mary Byrd Davis, Dave Foreman, Steve Gatewood, Reed Noss, Doug Scott, and Michael Soulé. Tom Butler, Jennifer Esser, Josh Brown, and Kevin Cross of *Wild Earth Journal*.

Musicians Steve Hulse, who produced *The Natural Sounds of Georgia*, and Anna Puccinelli, whose brother, Francis, introduced himself at the Oxford Conference for the Book and later sent me recordings of Anna's lovely piano compositions—their music has accompanied me through many a solitary hour of writing.

Leigh Feldman, never a double agent.

Franklin Ray and Lee Ada Branch Ray, who gave me life.

Silas, my true, and Susan, my constant. All my friends.

Raven, beloved, whose hand I can always feel at my back, like the wind lightly urging me onward.

And of course the wild places and their wild inhabitants,

which continue to sustain, comfort, inspire, and fascinate me.

This book is in memory of Judy Hancock, who devoted her life to a more livable, wilder world, and who never abandoned that vision. Judy, a resident of Lake City, Florida, and a fierce activist, was one of the Pinhook Corridor's truest friends. She died in 2004.

RESOURCES

POGO COALITION MEMBERS

FLORIDA WILDLIFE FEDERATION-POGO DIRECTOR
Manley Fuller
P. O. Box 6870
Tallahassee, Florida 32314-6870
(850) 656-7113
(850) 942-4431 fax
wildfed@aol.com
www.fwfonline.org

AUDUBON OF FLORIDA
Eric Draper
2507 Callaway Rd., Suite 103
Tallahassee, Florida 32303
(850) 224-7546 office
edraper@audubon.org
www.audubonofflorida.org

APALACHEE AUDUBON
Tallahassee, Florida
www.apalachee.org

DUVAL AUDUBON
Jacksonville, Florida
www.duvalaudubon.org

FLAGLER AUDUBON
Palm Coast, Florida
www. flaglerlibrary.org/audubon/audubon1.htm

FOUR RIVERS AUDUBON
Lake City, Florida

HALIFAX RIVER AUDUBON
Dayton Beach, Florida
www.halifaxriveras.org

SOUTHEAST VOLUSIA AUDUBON
Edgewater, Florida

MARION COUNTY AUDUBON
Orange Springs, Florida

ST. JOHNS COUNTY AUDUBON
St. Augustine, Florida
www.members.aol.com/sjaudubon/

DEFENDERS OF WILDLIFE
Laurie Macdonald
233 Third St. N. Suite 201
St Petersburg, Florida 33701
(727) 823-3888
(727) 823-3873 fax
lmacdonald@defenders.org
www.defenders.org

FLORIDA DEFENDERS OF THE ENVIRONMENT
Bob Simons
1122 SW 11th Ave.
Gainesville, Florida 32601
(352) 372-7646
rwsimons@bellsouth.net
www.fladefenders.org/index2.html

FLORIDA FEDERATION OF GARDEN CLUBS
Joan Pryor
1400 S. Denning Dr.
Winter Park, Florida 32789-5662

FLORIDA FEDERATION OF GARDEN CLUBS, DISTRICT IV
(NORTHEAST FLORIDA)
Marion Hilliard
2902 Greenridge Rd.
Orange Park, Florida 32073
(904) 264-6629
(904) 264-2440 fax
marionh@bellsouth.net

THE FLORIDA PANTHER SOCIETY
Stephen Williams & Karen C. Hill
Route 1 Box 1895
White Springs, Florida 32096
(386)397-2945
oldfla@atlantic.net
www.panthersociety.org/index.html

NATIONAL AUDUBON SOCIETY
Mike Daulton
1150 Connecticut Ave. NW, Suite 600
Washington, DC 20036
(202) 861-2242
mdaulton@audubon.org
www.audubon.org

NATIONAL WILDLIFE FEDERATION
Wes Woolf
1330 West Peachtree St. NW, Suite 475
Atlanta, Georgia 30309
(404) 876-8733 ext. 226
(404) 892-1744 fax
www.nwf.org

NORTH CAROLINA WILDLIFE FEDERATION
Larry Thompson, former director
P. O. Box 10626
Raleigh, North Carolina 27605
(919) 833-1923
ncwf_larry@mindspring.com

NORTH FLORIDA LAND TRUST
24 Cathedral Place, Suite 310
St. Augustine, Florida 32084

(904) 827-9870
nfltoffice@bellsouth.org
www.nflt.org

OKEFENOKEE ADVENTURES
Chip and Joy Campbell
Route 2 Box 3325
Folkston, Georgia 31537
(912) 496-7156
1 (866) THE-SWAMP
info@okefenokeeadventures.com
www.okefenokeeadventures.com

OKEFENOKEE BIRD CLUB
Sheila Willis
326 Pineview Dr.
Waycross, Georgia 31501
(912) 285-0419

OKEFENOKEE PASTIMES
Jo & Steve Knight
RR 2, Box 3090
Folkston, Georgia 31537
(912) 496-4472
(912) 496-4472 fax
swampufo@planttel.net
www.okefenokee.com

SIERRA CLUB FLORIDA REGIONAL OFFICE
475 Central Ave., M-1
St Petersburg, Florida 33701
(727) 824-8813
www.sierraclub.org

WILDERNESS SOCIETY
Frank Peterman & Shirl Parsons
112 Krog Street, Suite 26
Atlanta, Georgia 30307
(404) 872-9453 ext. 12
www.wilderness.org

Rare and Imperiled Species

The following animals and plants associated with the Okefenokee-Pinhook-Osceola Wildland Corridor are listed by federal or state (Florida or Georgia) governments as endangered, threatened, or species of special concern. More complete surveys will identify additional species.

Reptiles And Amphibians
American alligator
Gopher tortoise
Alligator snapping turtle
Striped mud turtle
Florida pine snake
Florida brown snake
Eastern ribbon snake
Eastern indigo snake
Gopher frog
Flatwoods salamander
Striped newt

Birds
Wood stork
White ibis
Red-cockaded woodpecker
Florida sandhill crane
Snowy egret
Tricolored heron
Little blue heron

Peregrine falcon
Southeastern American kestrel
Osprey
Bald eagle
Swallow-tailed kite
Bachman's sparrow
Bewick's wren

MAMMALS
Florida black bear
Sherman's fox squirrel

FISH
Blackbanded sunfish

PLANTS
Chapman's sedge
Large rosebud orchid
Hartwrightia
Pondspice
Florida toothache-grass
Parrot pitcher plant

ABOUT THE AUTHOR

 Naturalist and activist Janisse Ray is author of three books of literary non-fiction: the award-winning *Ecology of a Cracker Childhood* (Milkweed Editions, 1999), *Wild Card Quilt: Taking a Chance on Home* (Milkweed Editions, 2003), and *Pinhook: Finding Wholeness in a Fragmented Land* (Chelsea Green, 2005).

Ray's essays and poems have appeared in *Audubon*, *O: The Oprah Magazine*, *Orion*, *Natural History*, *Sierra*, and *Gray's Sporting Journal*. Her work is anthologized in *The Norton Anthology of Nature Writing*; *American Nature Writing 2000*; *The Best of Hope*; and *Where We Stand: Voices of Southern Dissent*, among others.

As an activist, Ray's work focuses on providing alternatives to industrial capitalism, slowing the rate of global warming, working to decelerate fragmentation, and making logging sustainable. She helped form the Georgia Nature-Based Tourism Association and worked to save the 3,400-acre Moody Forest in Appling, her home county. Ray is a founding board member of Altamaha Riverkeeper and is on the board of the Satilla Riverkeeper. She also organizes gatherings of southern nature writers.

Ray has been writer-in-residence at The Island Institute, Florida Gulf Coast University, the University of Mississippi, and Keene State College. Ray—with her husband, Raven Burchard, and their son, Silas—divides her time between Brattleboro, Vermont, and their family farm in southern Georgia.

CHELSEA GREEN PUBLISHING

the politics and practice of sustainable living

SUSTAINABLE LIVING has many facets. Chelsea Green's celebration of the sustainable arts has led us to publish trendsetting books about innovative building techniques, regenerative forestry, organic gardening and agriculture, solar electricity and renewable energy, local and bioregional democracy, and whole foods and Slow Food.

For more information about Chelsea Green, visit our Web site at www.chelseagreen.com, where you will find more than 200 books on the politics and practice of sustainable living.

Shelter

*The New Ecological Home:
A Complete Guide to
Green Building Options*
Daniel D. Chiras
ISBN 1-931498-16-4
$35.00

Planet

*What Can I Do?
An Alphabet for Living*
Lisa Harrow
ISBN 1-931498-66-0
$7.95

People

*This Organic Life:
Confessions of a Suburban
Homesteader*
Joan Dye Gussow
ISBN 1-931498-24-5
$16.95

Food

*The Slow Food Guide to
New York City:
Restaurants, Markets, Bars*
Patrick Martins &
Ben Watson
ISBN 1-931498-27-X
$20.00